A Heart Aflame

The Dynamics of Worship

by
James P. Gills, M.D.
St. Luke's Cataract and Intraocular Lens Institute

"To fall in love with God is the greatest of all romances.

To seek Him is the greatest of all adventures.

To find Him is the greatest human achievement."

—Author Unknown

To all who desire a deeper walk with the Lord.

With Love.

Table of Contents

Acknowledgments

To Tom and Theo Boylan of HeartLight Creative Services, I would like to express my sincere thanks for their editing and writing skills. This work unto the Lord has been greatly enhanced because of their faithfulness.

Acknowledgment

Part I

KINDLING THE FIRE

Chapter 1

Prelude to Worship

It was a cold, blustery evening in the midst of a northern winter. The temperature had already dipped below zero and the worst was yet to come. A man, heavily bundled, ventured forth into the nearly deserted street. To protect himself from the biting wind, he had wrapped his neck snugly with a warm scarf, except for the ends that flapped in the crisp night air. As he continued along to some unknown destination, the man spotted a neglected, shivering and half-starved dog seeking shelter behind a telephone pole.

Peering into the darkness the man saw that someone, in a cruel child's prank, had tied a tin can to the dog's tail. Struggling to loose itself from the can, it must have run from pillar to post. Finally, it could run no further. The poor mutt was completely entangled around the pole and stranded in the sub-zero weather. It was obvious that it would never survive on the street through such a night.

Coming closer, the man paused and looked the dog over. What a pitiful sight it was: thin, miserable, frightened, homeless and hungry. Compassion stirred, he yielded to the impulse of the moment. He stooped down, reached out his hand and called to the dog. Suspicious at first, and for good reason, the dog overcame its fears and gradually approached. Inch by slow inch it crept forward until it came under the man's hand. Gently, he patted and stroked the frightened animal, all the while speaking words of kindness. After removing the string from its tail, the man lifted the dog up, opened his overcoat and carefully tucked the bedraggled animal inside for the journey back home.

Finally, they arrived. As the man went into the house, he explained to his wife how he "found this half-starved

3

little dog on the street that would surely have died if left on its own out in the cold.''

"Please, sweetheart, put a blanket in the corner of the kitchen, by the stove where it's warm,'' the man urged, "and we'll take care of it at least for tonight.''

She smiled to herself, knowing his soft heart for strays. She returned with a suitable blanket and together they lovingly placed the still-quivering creature upon it. They offered a delicious bowl of warm milk and bread, followed by some scraps from the evening meal. The famished dog eagerly devoured it all. For the first time in many days the dog cautiously wagged its tail for the unusual kindness bestowed upon it.

The next day, as the man and his wife awoke to the early morning sunlight, the dog greeted its benefactors with a slightly more enthusiastic wag of its tail. As the couple exchanged a quick glance at one another, they reached a decision. The dog, though not much to look at in its present state, had found a home.

"What should we name him, dear?'' the man asked his wife. "He certainly must have a name if he's to be part of the family.'' They were both silent for a few moments, glancing at the dog and at each other.

"The way he looks now - **Old Bones** might be appropriate,'' the man's wife laughingly volunteered.

"It's true, he's not much of a prize right now,'' the man answered. "You just wait! In a month or so he'll look like he's got royal blood in him.'' He paused and thought a moment. "How about **Monarch?** Rather regal-sounding, don't you think? Besides, that's the name of a butterfly. You know how different *they* look from the ugly old caterpillar that spins a cocoon!'' So, Monarch it was.

Days and weeks passed since the new addition arrived in the family, revealing the incredible metamorphosis taking place in the old dog. His eyes became clearer, his nose grew cool and moist and his tail would wag whenever anyone even looked at him. More remarkable, though, was his coat. The silky, russet-colored fur glistened in the sunlight streaming in through the window onto his favorite napping spot. What a change in Monarch! As a result of good food and tender loving care, this fine-looking animal could scarcely be recognized as the same miserable stray of four weeks ago.

Each afternoon about four-thirty, Monarch would whine and scratch at the door to go outside. He would trot to the end of the walk, sit by the gate and wait for his master to come home from work. The sound of the family car coming up the street was etched clearly in his memory. As soon as the familiar noise reached his ears, he would begin barking excitedly and thumping his tail uncontrollably.

Such joy! Master was home! Then, when he heard the car door slam shut, Monarch could contain himself no longer. He ran in circles and bounded and leapt about, almost knocking the man over as he came through the gate. From that moment on, the two were inseparable for the rest of the evening.

The man relaxed in his favorite easy chair with his arm dangling lazily and Monarch slept contentedly at his side. Suddenly, something warm and wet nuzzling his hand startled the man awake. Leaning over, his gaze met two of the most loving, adoring eyes any dog ever had for his master. He nodded contentedly and smiled as, over and over, Monarch licked the hand of the one to whom he owed his very life. It was the same hand, in fact, that had reached out in far different circumstances not so long ago.

Above all else, one thing stood out in the scene. It was obvious that Monarch followed the man into the room out of sheer love and devotion. There was no begging for food or whining for attention, but mere gratitude at being able to rest at his master's side. Looking up with eyes filled with rapt adoration, and as the most intimate means of expressing the love he felt - licking the hand of his master, Monarch was content. (Based upon a story from *Worship*, by A.P. Gibbs)[1]

How well this little story portrays the essentials of worship! God desires that each of His children have a similar inner heart attitude. Not one of us can ever come to our Master on any terms other than that of being a doomed sinner, helplessly bound with the chains of the devil. We deserve only the wrath of a holy and righteous God, but instead, we are offered His ultimate expression of love.

Monarch differed from most of us in that *he knew* his master had saved his life. His only response in return was to freely express his feelings. Monarch's love for the man who had saved him from perishing was spontaneous and sincere. For many of us, it is more difficult to worship our Master who saved us. So often it involves a life-long process of learning to "let go."

How do we begin to cultivate an attitude of gratitude? Initially, we should look into the mysteries of our heart. God created man with a deep inner craving that He alone can fill. In fact, we were created for His pleasure, to worship Him,

> *"Now we were made to worship...All else fulfills its design; flowers are still fragrant and lilies are still beautiful and the bees still search for nectar amongst the flowers; the birds still sing with their thousand-voice choir on a summer's day, and the sun and the moon and the stars all move on their rounds doing the will of God.*
>
> *And from what we can learn from the Scriptures we believe that the seraphim and cherubim and powers and dominions are still fulfilling their design - worshipping God who also created them and breathed into them the breath of life. Man alone sulks in his cave. Man alone, with all of his brilliant intelligence, with all of his amazing, indescribable and wonderful equipment, still sulks in his cave.'"[2]*

How few have come to understand and accept man's intrinsic need to worship God! Only as we acknowledge the emptiness that cries for worship can the constant unrest within be settled. Our search for God will be most meaningful and effective when we realize our utter emptiness apart from Him.

The void within us is spiritual; yet, how often do we look to other areas of life in hope of finding the answer? Everyone is familiar with the busy executive who is ruthlessly driven to success after success, but is never satisfied. More often than not, this unbalanced lifestyle stems from an unrecognized, or purposely avoided, spiritual longing. To varying degrees, we are all guilty of seeking satisfaction through either intellectual, emotional, or physical stimulation. However, these rapidly fade away and leave us disillusioned and unfulfilled. Sadly enough, even after realizing that the one true Source of fulfillment is the living God, some may still not allow Him to do what He desires.

"There once was in man a true happiness of which now remains to him only the mark and empty trace, which he in vain tries to fill from all his surroundings, seeking from things absent the help he does not obtain in things present. But these are all inadequate, because the infinite abyss can only be filled by an infinite and immutable object, that is to say, only by God Himself."[3]

We are not alone in our avoidance of God. When we look to the children of Israel as our spiritual predecessors, we see this unfortunate fact occurring at Mt. Sinai. After God brought His people out of Egypt with one mighty miracle after another, He made them a most amazing offer. He asked them to enter into a personal relationship with Him. In God's words to Moses, and the Israelites' subsequent reply,

" 'You yourselves have seen what I did to the Egyptians, and how I bore you on eagles' wings, and brought you to Myself. Now then, if you will indeed obey My voice and keep My covenant, then you shall be My own possession among all the peoples, for all the earth is Mine; and you shall be to Me a kingdom of priests and a holy nation. These are the words that you shall speak to the sons of Israel.' "

Exodus 19:4-6

"And all the people perceived the thunder and the lightning flashes and the sound of the trumpet and the mountain smoking; and when the people saw it, they trembled and stood at a distance. Then they said to Moses, 'Speak to us yourself and we will listen; but let not God speak to us, lest we die.' And Moses said to the people, 'Do not be afraid; for God has come in order to test you, and in order that the fear of Him may remain with you, so that you may not sin.' "

Exodus 20:18-20

The people did not grasp the significance of God's invitation. They were offered the answer to their deep longing, but because of fear and lack of understanding, they preferred to remain at a distance. This is a point we must not overlook in our own lives.

Centuries later, in Jesus' conversation with a woman of Samaria, we see that neither the offer nor the response had changed. The woman's sexual promiscuity could no more fulfill the needy vacuum within her than could the mere obeying of the law for the Israelites.

> *"No man can meet a woman's spiritual needs, and a woman has not been born who can meet a man's spiritual needs. Our spirit belongs to God and can only find fulfillment and complete satisfaction in Him."* [4]

It is only as we worship, our spirit having been "released from captivity to soar in the presence of God," (Cornwall) that our "quiet desperation," as Thoreau called it, is satisfied.

This hunger within, then, is something that we must recognize and accept as having been placed within us by our Creator,

> *'Worship is written upon the heart of man by the hand of God...In a broad sense, worship is inseparable from and is an expression of life. It is not that man cannot live without worship, it is that he cannot fully live without worship...man was made to worship as surely as he was made to breathe. We may restrict the expression of worship for a season, just as we may briefly hold our breath, but there is an inward craving for worship that cannot be permanently stilled.'* [5]

Every attempt to seek satisfaction separate from God is futile. Our answer lies with the Lord of glory and in our worship of Him.

Even for the most dedicated Christian, living in this world of push-button conveniences and fast food chains can be challenging. Yet, we must remain free of the influence of these easy-come, easy-go philosophies if we are to develop a balanced love relationship with God. There are no shortcuts, but there are some keys that will unlock the door to our heart and kindle within each of us *"a heart aflame."*

How would we describe our walk with the Lord Jesus Christ? Could we say that we are passionately enthusiastic, alive and filled with the power of God? Are we zealously affected and glowing with a burning desire to be a godly person? Can we rest contentedly in the Lord's presence? These are questions we should all ask ourselves from time to time as a means of measuring the heart-fire of our love. Perhaps the flame is but dying embers, or has even gone out altogether. If so, let us consider this statement by A. W. Tozer, *"Worship* is the missing jewel of the evangelical church!"[6]

It is not enough that we have developed an intimate knowledge of God through His Word and have become committed to a covenant with Him. We may do both of these things and yet find, much to our dismay, that our heart is still not on fire. Something is missing - the zeal, the passion that is the sign of a true worshipper of God. A mature relationship with the Lord embodies all three of these components: a *knowledge* of Him, a *covenant* with Him, and *worship* of Him. These three represent the complete love of God. If the relationship is to grow in a healthy manner, they must be present in equal measure.

In my own personal search for worship, I went to many a Sunday service but failed to experience worship in my heart. Even in the Holy Land I found meaningful *places* to worship. Yet, I still lacked the ability to do so passionately. Finally, in my attempts to discover this elusive quality, I realized that the fault was not in the place. It was in me. I had to admit that I really did not know *how* to worship God.

What is worship and how may we define it? This is not an easy question to answer because worship involves nearly every aspect of our life. As a starting point, let us look to the Hebrew word "shachah" that is translated "worship" in the Old Testament of the Bible. It means "to depress or prostrate oneself as a means of paying homage, to bow, humbly beseech, do obeisance, do reverence, and to worship." We worship something when we pay it great honor and respect, when we consider it extremely precious, enough to adore. In the New Testament, the word is "proskuneo" which means "to kiss, (like a dog licking his master's hand); to fawn or crouch to, i.e. (literally or figuratively) prostrate one's self in homage (do reverence to, adore).''

Judson Cornwall drew a comparison between the meaning of the Old and New Testament words for worship, and how it is indicative of the difference between the old and new covenants,

> *"The word 'proskuneo' is far more descriptive than the*
> *Hebrew word 'shachah', for to the bowing is added*
> *kissing, and this requires close contact. We can bow at*
> *a distance, but kissing requires contact.''*[7]

In Webster's dictionary, worship is defined as "paying divine honor to God: a feeling of respect and a reverence for power, position, merit and virtue; dignity, worth, obsequious devotion and paying divine honor.''

The above definitions speak much about the external actions that may accompany worship, but little as to what is actually taking place in the heart. So, we must look at more definitions to broaden our understanding of this all-important activity. Worship is "glorifying God and enjoying Him forever" as stated in the catechism. Someone else described it as "a romance with God, an idealistic adventure of the extravagant and the mysterious in the spiritual realm.''

In his writings, A. W. Tozer approached worship as "a feeling in the heart, expressed in an appropriate way.'' He also stated that the "soul of the worshipper should be the most godlike thing in the universe.''[8] From worship comes an expansion of our intimate knowledge and covenant, which in turn enhances and reinforces our worship even further. Each one complements and completes the other two, but it is through worship that the fire is kindled.

William Temple, the late Archbishop of Canterbury, gave a beautiful description of worship in his book, *The Hope of a New World*,

> *"To worship is to quicken the conscience by the holiness*
> *of God, to feed the mind with the truth of God, to purge*
> *the imagination by the beauty of God, to open the heart*
> *to the love of God, to devote the will to the purpose of*
> *God.''*[9]

Worship is "practicing the presence of God" in anything we do, ✦ every time we do it (Brother Lawrence).

Granted, this may not be easy but the effects are both electrifying and fulfilling. That is just what worship should be: a "romance" with God. When we receive a revelation of our Savior's agitation of mind and spirit in Gethsemane, His fateful walk to Calvary, the agony He endured on the cross and His glorious resurrection, who could keep from responding with grateful adoration? Worship, then, is a joining with, and a rejoicing in, all that God is, all that He has done and all that He is yet to do.

A worshipper needs to experience these motivational feelings as he stands in awe and admiring fear to passionately and completely love God. Yet, being merely an occasional worshipper is far different from attaining a lifestyle of worship. According to John MacArthur, Jr., it "is not merely an activity to be injected into our schedules at certain intervals; rather, worship is itself a whole-life commitment, an all-encompassing response to Holy God..."[10] It is *worship as a way of life* for which we must strive. This is the key to spiritual transformation.

To practice the presence of God we must become intimately involved with the person of Jesus Christ. The special relationship and corresponding closeness that develop through the act of worship produce an obedience not possible in our own strength. Only a loving relationship with the Lord makes such submission and compliance attainable.

Worship, then, consists of a feeling in the heart stemming from the "humbling but delightful sense of admiring awe and astonishing wonder of the God of the universe."[11] These feelings must be expressed as an outward sign of an inward condition. Without emotion there can be no true worship, and without a lifestyle of worship there can be no true loving union with the Lord.

> *"If worship is love responding to love, and if nothing in heaven, on earth, or in hell can separate us from God's love, then surely nothing can separate us from responding to that love. That response is worship."*[12]

Chapter 2

The Love Triangles

The ideal relationship with God is comprised of three major elements: *knowledge* of Him, *worship* of Him and *covenant* with Him. No one element is more important than either of the other two; rather, they support one another. As an aid to understanding this concept, we will use an adaptation of Sternberg's love triangles of human relationships. Through these illustrations, we will see that it takes a balance to achieve the greatest possible love. Every interaction that a person experiences has, to one degree or another, the following components: cognizant, emotional and motivational factors. Each plays a vital part.

This triangle shows a perfect balance between the degree of intimacy, passion and commitment in a marital relationship. Such harmony should be our goal if we are to develop a healthy, fulfilling love that will grow, endure and produce lasting fruit. What exactly do we mean when we speak of intimacy, passion and commitment?

Intimacy

On the emotional side of the love triangle we have the degree of intimacy. The term ''intimacy'' here is comparable to that of "knowing" and means much more in the original Biblical languages. In both the Hebrew and Greek languages, "to know" implies a very intimate relationship best seen in a very close friendship. To understand our spouse in this manner does not come easily. It takes both time, effort and the sharing of many different experiences. As one's soul opens up to another's, there develops both a comradeship and mutual dependence that lend support during times of trouble.

Many people who have been divorced, in looking back at the factors that may have led to their break-up, realize that the level of intimacy had diminished gradually as the years drifted by. They made the mistake of not actively pursuing continued closeness in the relationship. As they grew in separate directions, they communicated less, shared fewer common interests, and finally divorced.

Passion

On the motivational side of the triangle we have the passion level in a relationship. Romance and physical union between husband and wife are essential components for a healthy love relationship between them. When they become "one flesh" in tender passion, it lends a uniqueness to their relationship that they have with no one else. Passion motivates them to greater commitment and leads to greater knowledge of their partner on a deeper level. It is passion that cements the whole relationship into one, cohesive bond. Trust is built, and feelings, not otherwise approachable, are expressed.

 Marriages that are based *entirely* on the passionate aspect often encounter many difficulties and end in disaster. These relationships are characterized by numerous and frequent partners, varying interests, loose living and consistently high rates of divorce. The volatile nature of passion causes it to burst forth quickly, but having no base, it ends up fading away.

A counterfeit of marital passion lies at the core of those high-school crushes and childhood infatuations we have all experienced. Consider the schoolboy who "falls in love" with the beautiful girl in one of his classes. Although thinking constantly of her, he never quite musters up enough courage to introduce himself and get to know her. Contrary to this, true passion is based on emotional intimacy with our spouse and involves total, devoted commitment.

Commitment

The cognizant side of the love triangle consists of the commitment present in the relationship. It develops on more of a straightforward course than either intimacy or passion and provides the strength necessary for the relationship to survive all the ups and downs in life. Commitment will grow or fail depending on how it is nurtured. In a husband and wife relationship, there must be absolute commitment on the part of each spouse to making the marriage a success, and to maintaining total fidelity. No allowance can be given for casual sexual encounters of any kind. This is the solid base upon which everything else is established. Another classic example of commitment is seen in the relationship between parent and child. Regardless of what the child may do, the parents' commitment never falters.

From the Human To The Divine

Ideally, every relationship would remain perfectly balanced, but in practice, such is not the case. Intimacy, passion and commitment will be present in varying degrees and change from time to time. In this section we will look at some of the combinations of these three elements that occur most frequently. An equilateral triangle (3 equal sides) is used to illustrate the model relationship. In those cases where imbalances are present, they will be represented by scalene, or unequal triangles. By making a comparison between human love and love for God, we will be better able to understand the role of worship in true spirituality.

Acquaintances

Acquaintances, which make up the majority of our interpersonal encounters, exhibit a noticeable lack of any of the three elements of love, as shown by the dotted lines. An example of a passing acquaintance would be a man who commutes on a train to work each morning. He exchanges greetings and small talk with others who take the same train on a regular basis. This is the extent of their relationship. Unfortunately, many people never develop more than casual acquaintances. At the root of this is often emotional or psychological problems, such as feelings of inferiority and fear of rejection.

In someone who is merely acquainted with God, there exists a similar situation. This person *knows about* the God of creation but does not love Him. He may even have joined a local church and sung worship songs with the rest of the congregation, but he does not have a relationship with the Lord. His is merely an acquaintance with Someone whom he does not know on an intimate basis, is not committed to, and therefore, cannot worship.

Cold Relationships

This variation of the human love relationship is one in which there is a strong commitment with very little intimacy and virtually no passion. If we restrict the divine flow of true intimacy and passion between spouses, the result is a relationship whose strength lies solely in the existence of the institution itself. It exists; therefore, it will continue to exist. This can sometimes be seen in prearranged marriages, or in couples where the fire of passion has been allowed to go out.

In looking at a cold relationship with God, we see one important fact. Regardless of the varying levels of knowledge and covenant, there is virtually no worship. This imbalance occurs for many reasons, but primarily because of cultural or doctrinal restraints. Far too common today is the cold church that does not worship the

God they serve. Even sadder is the church that once experienced true worship, but has now lost that ability. As our Lord Jesus Himself said to the church at Ephesus,

> *"But I have this against you, that you have left your first love."*

Revelation 2:4

There are several ways in which a cold relationship with God may develop. The first example shows an overabundance of covenantal commitment, some knowledge, and minimal worship. The people here are often committed to the habit of their religion, but do not really know what they believe or why they believe as they do. We should not fail to mention, though, that there are benefits to having a strong commitment. These churches may have developed a ritual that will hold them together if all else fails. Yet, we should never mistake this formalized behavior for true worship. In those cases where the change from worship to ritual has taken place, there is a stern warning from the Lord. He will take away the glory of His presence,

> *"Remember therefore from where you have fallen, and repent and do the deeds you did at first; or else I am coming to you, and will remove your lampstand out of its place - unless you repent."*

Revelation 2:5

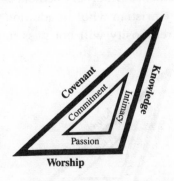

The second example shows more of a balance between knowledge and covenant, but with worship still at a minimum. As a result, it is impossible for God's heart of compassion to thaw the ice and kindle within the people a heart aflame. Without the fire of worship, it is all too easy to become judgmental or critical. For instance, we may look down upon those who do not have the same level of Biblical knowledge, or as many verses memorized. We may criticize those who are not participating in as many service-oriented projects. The result: still a cold Christian.

In the third variation of the cold relationship with God, knowledge has become the predominant factor. Intellectuals who have much knowledge of the Word of God, less than optimum covenant and again, minimal worship typify these churches. We should never pursue knowledge for its sake alone. Its path leads only to legalism and self-righteous piety. Two well-known Biblical examples are the Scribes and Pharisees of Jesus' day.

It is not enough to possess mere intellectual assent and to give an external show of obedience. Internal obedience must be complete or the result may be a Christian who, in addition to being cold, is disobedient. External religiosity will not pass the test.

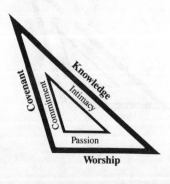

Warm Relationships

As we consider the warm relationship between two people we find a high level of intimacy. This situation has as its strongest points the shared emotional experiences and the results they produce. Common experiences between spouses, even tragic ones, bring about a closeness and mutual dependence that lend support. As they exchange thoughts and ideas the level of communication rises. All in all, there is very little passion in these relationships and the result is more of a companionship that endures even after the physical attraction has faded.

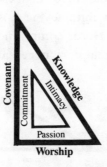

The warm love of God relationship is characterized by much knowledge of His Word, some covenant-commitment and very little worship. Christians in this category read their Bibles, identify with and memorize many verses, but fail to grow in their worship. They know Jesus through His Word and may even have a degree of complacent friendship with Him, but their hearts are not ablaze. God's warning regarding lukewarm Christianity should not be taken lightly by any of us,

> *"So because you are lukewarm, and neither hot nor cold, I will spit you out of My mouth."*
>
> Revelation 3:16

Hot Relationships

Hot relationships have passion as the strongest ingredient. When it is teamed up with intimacy, a form of romantic love takes place.

This "Romeo and Juliet" kind of love is most often seen in summer affairs that occur among young adults.

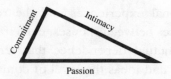

A second form of hot love occurs when passion and commitment are very strong, but intimacy is missing. Sternberg labeled this "Hollywood love." Here, commitment is based solely on passion and lacks the emotional core necessary to endure the test of time.

Inherent in the hot relationship is a cycle that begins on a highly positive note and then swings in the opposite direction. This period of on-again, off-again, or hot-cold, will usually continue for a brief time. If it persists, it will develop a highly negative factor. What began in the heat of passion winds up on the ice of contempt.

This is not to say that passion is wrong. Hugging, kissing and making love within the bonds of marriage are very much a part of God's plan. In the proper balance and at the appropriate time they enhance the desire for renewed commitment and even greater intimacy.

Hot relationships occur also in our love of God. In the first example there is an overabundance of worship with less emphasis placed on the teaching of His Word, and the necessary obedience to it.

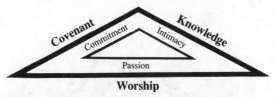

The Christian who has this kind of relationship with the Lord will come to church to experience an emotional "high" from the congregational worship. He is in constant danger of trying to live from one "high" to the next. Such artificiality is very unhealthy.

Another variation of the hot relationship is one in which the level of knowledge approaches the degree of worship, but the covenant relationship with God has not been firmly established. Churches of this nature experience superior worship. They seek higher revelations of God, but are ultimately unable to make the transition from mere intellectual knowledge to practical commitment.

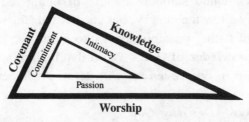

Without the deep commitment involved in covenant, the values of faith, trust and belief become empty. When carried to extremes, this lack may lead to doubting even the deity of God. These fellowships are characterized by gradual up and down swings and hold a particular attraction for Christians who have left other churches. As a result, there is a high rate of congregational turnover. Even in those cases where there is an explosion of church growth, there is a high rate of instability.

The hot Christians who are attracted by these churches often exhibit a lack of commitment in their personal lives, as well. They may be more apt to seek divorce when marital problems arise and their overall work habits may be far less than optimum. These loving, outgoing Christians know God and truly love to worship Him. Unfortunately, they are not quite able to make a commitment to total obedience.

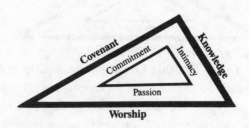

The third example of a hot relationship with God is one lacking knowledge. These churches, and the people who frequent them, are both committed to, and love worshipping, a God whom they do not know very well. Therefore they are unable to be totally directed by God and stand in danger of being led astray. This deficiency may allow the hungry, but uneducated Christian to wander along aberrant paths, possibly even into cults.

It is our *knowledge* of God's Word that maintains the accuracy of our *worship* in our *covenant* with Him. All facets of the love relationship are of equal importance. As John Piper expressed so well in his book, *Desiring God*,

> *"Truth without emotion produces dead orthodoxy and a church full (or half-full) of artificial admirers (like people who write generic anniversary cards for a living). On the other hand, emotion without truth produces empty frenzy and cultivates shallow people who refuse the discipline of rigorous thought. But true worship comes from people who are deeply emotional and who love deep and sound doctrine. Strong affections for God rooted in truth are the bone and marrow of Biblical worship.* "[13]

For our love to evolve into all that God ordained, it is essential that we achieve and maintain the proper balance. Of supreme importance is the love relationship that we develop with God through Jesus Christ. Upon this union with Him will every other activity be based. All other relationships will only be as strong and fulfilling as the one we have with Him.

In concluding this presentation, let us return once again to A. W. Tozer's statement, "Worship is the missing jewel of the evangelical church." Can we make a determination as to which love triangle would be applicable to his statement? It is the one with its two longest sides being fairly equal in knowledge and covenant, but with very little worship. Many believe these churches are suffering a decline in membership, despite high levels of both commitment and knowledge, because of a lack of true worship. The motivational component is sadly missing from their curriculum. Therefore, everyone suffers. Let us set out in search of this precious gem and once found, restore its rightful place.

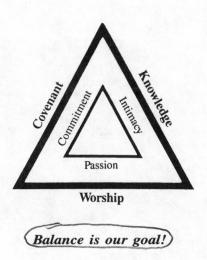

Balance is our goal!

Chapter 3

Making Ready the Heart

When *God measures a man He puts a tape around the heart instead of the head''* (author unknown). There are some prerequisites to entering into this worship experience with God. The unregenerate man cannot receive spiritual wisdom and therefore, is incapable of worship. Only those who have been brought into a living, vital relationship with God the Father through Jesus Christ are capable of true worship. In fact, as Chuck Swindoll taught in a message on worship, ''The only person *justified* in not worshipping is the unbeliever. For to worship you have to have a Savior, and your Savior has to be the central figure of your life.''[14] (emphasis mine) Jesus said to the Pharisee Nicodemus,

> *"Truly, truly, I say to you, unless one is born again, he cannot see the kingdom of God."*
> John 3:3

For those who have entered into this Father-son relationship, God gives the divine directive to love Him in the first two of the ten commandments (Exodus 20:1,2). Also, in the words of the Lord Jesus, Himself,

> *"You shall love the Lord your God with all your heart, with all your soul, and with all your mind. This is the great and foremost commandment."*
> Matthew 22:37,38

Do these commands imply the fervent and passionate expression of our knowledge of God? Are they mandates for a burning dedication of our lives to Him above all else? Yes! To both of these questions - a resounding yes! Knowing this, we face a choice. Once we hear Him knocking, we must decide whether or not to open the door - not only at the moment of salvation, but throughout our growing relationship with Him.

> *"Behold, I stand at the door and knock; if anyone hears My voice and opens the door, I will come in to him, and will dine with him, and he with Me."*
>
> Revelation 3:20

In choosing to open more and more of our heart and "dine" with the Lord Jesus, we have made the most important of all decisions. From this point on, every choice will present either an obstacle or an opportunity for the Lord. Decisions related to employment, a companion, or a place to live are subject to other people. We actually have only one true choice, whether or not we will worship the Lord. Sadly enough, it is one most of us never make. Each of us must ask, "Am I willing to respond to God?"

How does one worship? For years I have wanted to know the answer to this question and I have searched for it in many ways. There has always existed within me a hunger to be filled with more of God. Though I have done some strange things in learning, I have discovered that only true, heart-felt worship can satisfy that hunger.

Some basic heart attitudes must be cultivated before we can ever begin to worship the Lord, the most important of which is humility. A humble heart is not something that comes naturally. Yet, to become a worshipper, it is essential.

> *"Humble yourselves, therefore, under the mighty hand of God, that He may exalt you at the proper time."*
>
> I Peter 5:6

We must be broken before the presence of God, and be willing to take on His thoughts even as our Lord did,

> *"Have this attitude in yourselves which was also in Christ Jesus, who, although He existed in the form of God, did*

not regard equality with God a thing to be grasped,
but emptied Himself, taking the form of a bond-servant,
and being made in the likeness of men. And being found
in appearance as a man, He humbled Himself by becoming
obedient to the point of death, even death on a cross."

Philippians 2:5-8

Mary of Bethany demonstrated the heart attitudes to which we are referring,

"Mary therefore took a pound of very costly perfume of
pure nard, and anointed the feet of Jesus, and wiped
His feet with her hair; and the house was filled with the
fragrance of the perfume."

John 12:3

This expression of her love and gratitude to Jesus cost approximately a year's earnings, but her heart was so completely "sold out" to the Savior that the cost of her gift did not matter. She desired no half-measures with which to express her devotion, but gave her all. Let us not entertain the thought that worshipping is easy or that it is just a song we sing. "The path of wholehearted discipleship has never been crowded, or popular."[15]

How true this is! As we embark on the road to becoming dedicated worshippers, our actions will undoubtedly be as misunderstood and questioned as were Mary's,

"But Judas Iscariot, one of His disciples, who was
intending to betray Him, said, 'Why was this perfume not
sold for three hundred denarii, and given to poor
people?'"

John 12:4

When we are criticized, let us take comfort from the words of our Lord. It certainly was not that He lacked compassion on the poor, for His whole life showed His love for the outcasts, and His command was to take care of them. However, He replied to Judas' query,

"Let her alone, in order that she may keep it for the day of My burial. For the poor you always have with you, but you do not always have Me."

John 12:7

Mary was not swayed from her belief in Jesus as the Messiah by the skepticism of those around her. By her unreserved act of love, she was the only one to hold the honor of having anointed Jesus for His burial. Can we, like Mary of Bethany, give our sacrificial best to Him?

Jesus agonized, cried and wept for the presence of God. Is it right to think that we need do any less? We must constantly hunger after God's presence, guard against becoming downcast or indifferent, and through it all, remain humble. As we are humbled, we will in turn begin to acknowledge the greatness of God until finally, these two separate acts become one. If we can but catch a glimpse of our God as He truly is, then our lives will gain the proper perspective. Can we seek to declare with David,

"O Lord, our Lord, How majestic is Thy name in all the earth. Who hast displayed Thy splendor above the heavens! When I consider Thy heavens, the work of Thy fingers, the moon and the stars, which Thou has ordained; What is man, that Thou dost take thought of him? And the son of man, that Thou dost care for him?"

Psalm 8:1,3,4

How natural this should be! Only when we are truly humble can we fully appreciate the majesty of our God. Yet, at the same time, we can never achieve such a heart attitude of humility *until* we see the Lord as He really is. A divine revelation of the magnificence and absolute holiness of God causes brokenness and humility. These attitudes should motivate us to worship Him passionately, rather than draw back, cringing in fear. It may seem that we have reached an impasse with these apparent contradictions, or antinomies. How can we be humble enough to see God without having seen Him, or to be broken and yet, full of zeal?

What can we do to resolve this dilemma and begin to worship?

In our own strength - nothing. Aside from deciding to become a worshipper and to seek God with our whole heart, it is beyond our control. We can only wait upon God to supernaturally reveal Himself as He did with the prophet Isaiah,

> *"...I saw the Lord sitting on a throne, lofty and exalted, with the train of His robe filling the temple. Then I said, 'Woe is me, for I am ruined! Because I am a man of unclean lips; And I live among a people of unclean lips; For my eyes have seen the King, the Lord of hosts.' "*
>
> Isaiah 6:1,5

Isaiah did not merely sit and wait. Our waiting, like his, should be active and not passive. We may rest assured that, as we turn our heart fully toward God, it is His desire to reveal Himself in order that we might worship Him,

> *"And you will seek Me and find Me, when you search for Me with all your heart."*
>
> Jeremiah 29:13

Time after time, the Scriptures reveal the Lord of Glory through the eyes of Holy Spirit-inspired servants of old. As we look into the Word, let us keep in mind that the same Spirit is waiting to lead us to a wealth of truth that is accessible only through Him. Why not, before continuing, ask Him to open the eyes of our understanding that we may also know the glory of the one true God?

Part II

THE

BLAZE

BUILDS

Chapter 4

Visions of Glory

T *hine, O Lord, is the greatness and the power and the glory and the victory and the majesty, indeed everything that is in the heavens and the earth; Thine is the dominion, O Lord, and Thou dost exalt Thyself as head over all. Both riches and honor come from Thee, and Thou dost rule over all, and in Thy hand is power and might; and it lies in Thy hand to make great, and to strengthen everyone. Now therefore, our God, we thank Thee, and praise Thy glorious name.''*

I Chronicles 29:11-13

King David, described as a man after God's own heart, expressed so well in those few lines the key to true worship. Through all the trials he had endured in his life, David came to know something of the great God he served. Only from the lips of someone who truly loved God could these beautiful phrases have sprung forth,

> *"As the deer pants for the water brooks, so my soul pants for Thee, O God. My soul thirsts for God, for the living God; When shall I come and appear before God?''*

Psalm 42:1-2

As we now look at three visions of His glory, may God begin to develop within each one of us this same heart of love! The Apostle John, while in exile on the isle of Patmos, received the following vision of the Lord in His heavenly realm. The first passage is one in which God manifests Himself as the eternal Creator. He has existed forever and will continue to exist; it was for His own pleasure that the universe was created.

> *"Immediately I was in the Spirit: and behold, a throne was standing in heaven, and One sitting on the throne. And He who was sitting was like a jasper stone and a sardius in appearance; and there was a rainbow around the throne, like an emerald in appearance...And from the throne proceed flashes of lightning and sounds and peals of thunder. And there were seven lamps of fire burning before the throne, which are the seven Spirits of God.*"
>
> Revelation 4:2,3,5

This throne is not just an ordinary throne, but that of the living God. It is surrounded by an emerald rainbow, lightning and fire. God is not alone; the twenty-four elders and all the heavenly servants surround His throne and worship Him continually.

> *"...and day and night they do not cease to say, Holy, Holy, Holy, is the Lord God, the Almighty, who was and who is and who is to come. And when the living creatures give glory and honor and thanks to Him who sits on the throne, to Him who lives forever and ever, the twenty-four elders will fall down before Him who sits on the throne, and will worship Him who lives forever and ever, and will cast their crowns before the throne, saying, Worthy art Thou, our Lord and our God, to receive glory and honor and power; for Thou didst create all things, and because of Thy will they existed, and were created.*"
>
> Revelation 4:8-11

This scene, with the twenty-four elders, points toward the first covenant with the children of Israel and to the new covenant with the Gentiles. Many believe that twelve of the twenty-four represent the patriarchs of the tribes of Israel. The other twelve may be the apostles of Jesus, indicating the turning point in God's relationship with man. He is a holy God who always was, and always will be, worthy of glory and honor. If He is worthy of continuous adoration from all the hosts of heaven, how much more should we, His children, worship Him here on earth?

As we read John's vision, we might notice that God was, and still is seated. He doesn't appear the least bit anxious about the direction things have taken in His creation. For those who fear, because of present situations and circumstances, that God has lost control, this fact is reassuring. We can draw much comfort in these troubled times. God reigns supreme. Everything proceeds according to His divine direction.

In the next heavenly portrait the hosts of both heaven and earth were worshipping God for His provision. As the drama unfolded, John wept because no man in, on, or under the earth was found worthy to open and read the book with seven seals. One of the elders comforted him, and then showed him this truth,

> *"And one of the elders said to me, 'Stop weeping; behold the Lion that is from the tribe of Judah, the Root of David, has overcome so as to open the book and its seven seals.' And I saw between the throne (with the four living creatures) and the elders a Lamb standing, as if slain, having seven horns and seven eyes, which are the seven Spirits of God, sent out into the earth. And He came, and He took it out of the right hand of Him who sat on the throne."*
>
> Revelation 5:5-7

Jesus Christ is the Lamb of God, the only One worthy to be a sacrifice for the redemption of all. Thus, He is worthy of our worship,

> *"And they sang a new song, saying, 'Worthy art Thou to take the book, and to break its seals; for Thou wast slain, and didst purchase for God with Thy blood men from every tribe and tongue and people and nation.' "*
>
> Revelation 5:9

At the close, John witnessed the most tremendous worship scene of all time. Let us stand with him and experience the wonder of it,

> *"And I looked, and I heard the voice of many angels around the throne and the living creatures and the elders; and the number of them was myriads of myriads, and thousands of thousands, saying with a loud voice, 'Worthy is the Lamb that was slain to receive power and riches and wisdom and might and honor and glory and blessing.' "*
>
> Revelation 5:11,12

Picture for a moment, standing among the countless multitudes as they join together to praise the God who gave His life for His creation. How magnificent must be the sound of "thousands of thousands" of voices raised to the glory of God! Could anyone remain silent on such a wondrous occasion? Our God reigns, and the Lamb with Him!

God's glorious plan also revealed to John, Jesus Christ as the Mighty Conqueror, our soon-coming King. This referred to the second coming of the Messiah. No longer was He portrayed as the Lamb, but as a King coming to claim His rightful inheritance,

> *"And I saw heaven opened; and behold, a white horse, and and He who sat upon it is called Faithful and True; and in righteousness He judges and wages war. And His eyes are a flame of fire, and upon His head are many diadems; and He has a name written upon Him which no one knows except Himself. And He is clothed with a robe dipped in blood; and His name is called The Word of God. And the armies which are in heaven, clothed in fine linen, white and clean, were following Him on white horses. And from His mouth comes a sharp sword, so that with it He may smite the nations; and He will rule them with a rod of iron and He treads the wine press of the fierce wrath of God, the Almighty. And on His robe and on His thigh He has a name written, "King of Kings, and Lord of Lords."*
>
> Revelation 19:11-16

Hallelujah! There can be no mistaking this message. Jesus is the King of Kings and the Lord of Lords. When He returns with His army there will be total victory. We have this assurance from God Himself. The devil's time of torment will come to an end; indeed, by faith, has come to an end already. Can we see why John saw God seated on the throne and not nervously "wringing His hands?" Jesus will exact judgment upon those who rejected the free gift He offered. He is the living Word and that Word will judge the world. Satan, the fallen angels and those he has deceived will burn in the lake of fire forever. We worship God, then, because we have escaped this second everlasting death and been inducted into the heavenly army to serve as priests and kings.

Yes, there is victory in Jesus! What began with creation, was seen in the Old Testament and fulfilled in the New Testament will be brought to a close when the King returns. His ways are higher than our ways, and His thoughts higher than our thoughts (Isaiah 55:9). We will not always understand all that takes place around us, but God is faithful.

If we love God above all else He gives us the promise,

*"And we know that **God causes all things to work together for good** to those who love God, to those who are called according to His purpose."*

Romans 8:28

How sure are the promises of God? How dependable is His Word?

"For as the rain and the snow come down from heaven, and do not return without watering the earth, and making it bear and sprout, and furnishing seed to the sower and bread to the eater; so shall My word be which goes forth from My mouth; It shall not return to Me empty, without accomplishing what I desire, and without succeeding in the matter for which I sent it."

Isaiah 55:10,11

How can we do anything less than offer high praises to our God for such precious and powerful promises? Will we join with King David and declare the glory of the Lord whom he loved so much? He alone is worthy!

Chapter 5

Getting to Know the God We Worship

I t is important to know all we can of the One who created us, loved and died for us, and waits for the fulfillment of all things. Have we ever asked ourselves the question, "Who is this God that I serve?" What comes to mind when someone speaks of Jesus Christ? Does He take on some specific form or shape? If these questions were asked of a group of people, there would undoubtedly be many differing descriptions, some of a sound Scriptural basis and some, otherwise. A. W. Tozer stated that our most important thought is our conception of God. Therefore, it must be as close as possible to the truth. Only then can we "worship Him in Spirit and in truth."

We may uncover a wealth of insight into the nature of God by looking at His many different names. In the Hebrew language a name was of much more significance than in the United States today. It expressed the nature, or character, of that which it named. To pursue our understanding of who God is, we can best begin with *how He revealed Himself* to the children of Israel through many of His names.

Elohim

In the first verse of the first chapter of the first book of the Bible, it is written, "God created..." The word for God here is Elohim, and in it are the first clues to God's identity. Elohim is plural (an indication of His triune nature), and declares His supremacy as the Creator. The One we worship is the "eternal, immortal, invisible, the only wise

39

God'' (I Timothy 1:17). He is the Father, Son and Holy Spirit; He is *our* Father, *our* Lord, and the Spirit living in every believer.

> *"The worship of the eternal God through His eternal Spirit is far more than merely touching eternity; it is actually entering into an activity that is eternal in every dimension...Worshippers reach from before the world until after the world and join the angels of heaven in worship and adoration of God, 'the Alpha and the Omega, the Beginning and the End...who is and who was and who is to come, the Almighty.' "*[16]

In a message on worship, Anne Graham Lotz described God as being Eternity, Divinity and Activity. God is eternal, and therefore, not bound by the restrictions of time. He is timeless and exists outside of time itself. As the Apostle Peter noted, a thousand years may be as one day in His sight. In addition to, and possibly as a result of, God's timelessness, He is not bound by space. In His omnipresence and omniscience, He is present always and everywhere. He sees and knows all things.

There was only one occasion when God limited Himself to the boundaries of time, and He did that for us! God chose to become a part of His creation in order to redeem it. When Jesus came in the flesh, He lived by the exact same rules by which He expected man to live. Then the Lord went one step further. He submitted Himself to His own creation and allowed it to crucify Him, that we might live.

God expressed His divinity through creation, but He is much greater than anything in it. Elohim created all and controls all, yet, is as separate from His creation as an artist from his painting. As the painting on canvas is a reflection of the artist, so is the universe only a mere reflection of the Creator.

When we speak of the activity of God, we are referring to God, the Creator as we see Him in the opening chapters of Genesis and the first chapter of John. Our Lord Jesus (the Word) is the active part of the Trinity,

*"In the beginning was the Word, and the Word was with
God, and the Word was God. He was in the beginning
with God. All things came into being by Him, and apart
from Him nothing came into being that has come into
being."*

John 1:1-3

Let us worship Him, the eternal Creator, Elohim!

El Shaddai

This name appears in Genesis 17:1 as a declaration by God to
Abram. He said, "I am El Shaddai: Almighty God." Here is the
combination of God's great and glorious nature (El) with His ability
to provide. A close approximation of the meaning of Shaddai is that
of a mother's breast. In the same way that a mother's breast satisfies,
nourishes and comforts her baby, so does our God do for us. He
is mighty toward us in His ability to comfort, feed and satisfy.

We should note that only after God declared Himself as El
Shaddai, did He establish the covenant with Abram and change his
name to Abraham. God was, in essence, stating His ability to fulfill
His part in the relationship with Abraham and all of his descendants.
Up until this time, God was known as the Creator in an impersonal
sort of way, but with this covenant, things changed. A unique
relationship began and a new revelation of the nature of God was
unveiled.

Let us worship Him, Almighty God, El Shaddai!

Jehovah-Jireh

The meaning of this name can be found in the passage where
God commanded Abraham to offer his precious, long-awaited son
as a sacrifice. The Lord required such obedience from Abraham as
a means of testing, or proving, his faithfulness. Abraham needed
to learn to trust God implicitly as El Shaddai. Would God provide
a means for his son Issac to return with him from the mount?
Abraham's words to his servants even before climbing the mount
of sacrifice showed his faith in God's ability to do so,

*"On the third day Abraham raised his eyes and saw the place from a distance. And Abraham said unto his young men, 'Stay here with the donkey, and I and the lad will go yonder; and **we will worship and return to you.**' "*

Abraham's confidence in El Shaddai never wavered. He may not have known the details of how Issac would survive, but he knew that God would be faithful to His former promises. As we read further on, it is evident that God was, and is, calmly in control. All He required was Abraham's unquestioning obedience,

"And Abraham stretched out his hand, and took the knife to slay his son. But the angel of the Lord called to him from heaven, and said, 'Abraham, Abraham!' And he said, 'Here I am.' And He said, 'Do not stretch out your hand against the lad, and do nothing to him; for now I know that you fear God, since you have not withheld your son, your only son, from Me.' Then Abraham raised his eyes and looked, and behold, behind him a ram caught in the thicket by his horns; and Abraham went and took the ram, and offered him up for a burnt offering in the place of his son. And Abraham called the name of that place (Jehovah-jireh), the Lord will provide, as it is said to this day, 'In the mount of the Lord it will be provided.' "

Genesis 22:10-14

This great act of faith was but a foreshadowing of another Father who would one day offer His only Son. Let us worship Him, the Lord our provider, Jehovah-jireh!

Jehovah-Nissi

This name means, "the Lord our banner." After their miraculous deliverance from Egypt, the children of Israel were confronted by the Amalekites. This first battle was the scene where God revealed Himself as Jehovah-nissi,

"So Moses said to Joshua, 'Choose men for us, and go out, fight against Amalek. Tomorrow I will station myself on the top of the hill with the staff of God in my hand.' And Joshua did as Moses told him, and fought against Amalek; and Moses, Aaron, and Hur went up to the top of the hill. So it came about when Moses held his hand up that Israel prevailed, and when he let his hand down, Amalek prevailed. But Moses' hands were heavy. Then they took a stone and put it under him, and he sat on it; and Aaron and Hur supported his hands, one on one side and one on the other. Thus his hands were steady until the sun set. So Joshua overwhelmed Amalek and his people with the edge of the sword. Then the Lord said to Moses, 'Write this in a book as a memorial, and recite it to Joshua, that I will utterly blot out the memory of Amalek from under heaven.' And Moses built an altar, and named it (Jehovah-nissi) the Lord is my banner."

Exodus 17:9-15

Each time Moses held up the rod of God, the people were able to overcome the enemy. When the rod came down they lost ground. This rod, then, was the standard to which the people rallied, and when it was raised, God performed miracles to insure victory. Symbolic of God Himself, the rod pointed forward through the ages to Jesus. Like Moses, who built an altar to commemorate God's name, we should never forget that God is our banner. We rally to Jehovah-nissi, and exalt Him who "always causes us to triumph" (II Corinthians 2:14).

Let us worship Him, the Lord our banner, Jehovah-nissi!

Jehovah-Rophe

After the children of Israel crossed the Red Sea, they were in the wilderness without water for three days. When they finally found some it was too bitter to drink. Once again, God proved that He was truly their provider. Through the miraculous, He confirmed this new revelation of His nature as their healer, Jehovah-rophe,

"So the people grumbled at Moses, saying 'What shall we drink?' Then he cried out to the Lord, and the Lord showed him a tree; and he threw it into the waters, and the waters became sweet. There He made for them a statute and regulation, and there He tested them. And He said, 'If you will give earnest heed to the voice of the Lord your God, and do what is right in His sight, and give ear to His commandments, and keep all His statutes, I will put none of the diseases on you which I have put on the Egyptians; for I, the Lord, am (Jehovah-rophe) your healer.' "

Exodus 15:24-26

Let us worship Him, the Lord our healer, Jehovah-rophe!

Jehovah-Shalom

This name means "the Lord our peace." It was revealed to Gideon at a crucial point in his life. During this period in history, the people of Israel were experiencing hard times and cried out for deliverance. God responded to their cry by sending an angel to tell Gideon he had been chosen to be the instrument of their release. After learning of his high calling and of God's assurance to be with him, Gideon offered a present to the Lord. When it was made ready it was consumed by fire that sprang out of the rock upon which it lay,

"When Gideon saw that he was an angel of the Lord, he said, 'Alas, O Lord God! For now I have seen the angel of the Lord face to face.' And the Lord said to him, 'Peace to you, do not fear; you shall not die.' Then Gideon built an altar there to the Lord and named it (Jehovah-shalom) the Lord is peace."

Judges 6:22-24

This revelation came at a time of national unrest and in the face of insurmountable odds. It is the same for us today. No matter what circumstances we face, despite how things look, or how we feel in the midst of turmoil, we have a wonderful assurance. Our peace does not depend upon anyone or anything. God *is* our peace. Let us worship Him, the Lord our peace, Jehovah-shalom!

Jehovah-Tsidkenu

God gave us this name, "the Lord our righteousness," in a prophetic word to Jeremiah. All our own righteous deeds are as "filthy rags" before a holy God, as the Word reminds us in Isaiah 64:6.

> " *'Behold, the days are coming,' declares the Lord, when I will raise up for David a righteous Branch, and he will reign as king and act wisely, and do justice and righteousness in the land. In His days Judah will be saved, and Israel will dwell securely: and this is His name by which he will be called, (Jehovah-tsidkenu) The Lord our righteousness.' "*
>
> Jeremiah 23:5,6

Jehovah-tsidkenu pointed forward to the coming of Jesus as the perfect Lamb of God. We find in the writing of the apostle Paul that Jesus, who knew no sin, was made sin that we might become the righteousness of God in Him (II Corinthians 5:21).

Let us worship Him, the Lord our righteousness, Jehovah-tsidkenu!

Jehovah-M'kaddesh

Here we find another facet of God's nature, later made manifest in the Son of God - Jehovah-m'kaddesh, the Lord our sanctifier. God gave a commandment to Moses,

> *"But as for you, speak to the sons of Israel, saying, 'You shall surely observe My sabbaths; for this is a sign between Me and you throughout your generations, that you may know that I am (Jehovah-m'kaddesh) the Lord who sanctifies you.' "*
>
> Exodus 31:13

It is tremendously important that we realize it is our God who sanctifies us, not we ourselves, and this, through the blood of our Savior. "Therefore Jesus also, that He might sanctify the people through His own blood..." (Hebrews 13:12) "And such were some of you; but you were washed, but you were sanctified, but you were justified in the name of the Lord Jesus Christ, and in the Spirit of our God" (I Corinthians 6:11). We have only to accept what Jesus already accomplished on the cross.

Let us worship Him, the Lord our sanctifier, Jehovah-m'kaddesh!

Jehovah-Shammah

In the book of Ezekiel, God revealed Himself to the prophet as Jehovah-shammah, the Lord is present. Ezekiel had a vision of the Holy City that is to be established upon the new earth at the close of the age. This New Jerusalem will be God's dwelling place forever,

> "The city shall be 18,000 cubits round about; and the name of the city from that day shall be, (Jehovah-shammah), the Lord is there."

> Ezekiel 48:35

This speaks of a future event, but it is applicable to us today. God still meets with man in His tabernacle (temple). We, the members of His Body, are living temples in which His Holy Spirit dwells (I Corinthians 3:16). Jesus promised in Matthew 28:20, "...lo, *I am with you always*, even to the end of the age. On that glorious day we will walk the streets of New Jerusalem and see God face to face.

Let us worship Him, the Lord is present, Jehovah-shammah!

Jehovah-Rohi

Almost everyone is familiar with that great psalm of King David in which he declared, "The Lord is my shepherd; I shall not want" (Psalm 23:1). Jesus reminds us who this shepherd is,

"I am the good shepherd: the good shepherd lays down his life for the sheep. He who is a hireling, and not a shepherd, who is not the owner of the sheep, beholds the wolf coming, and leaves the sheep, and flees, and the wolf snatches them, and scatters them."

John 10:11,12

Without a leader to follow, we are like sheep who so easily go astray. Jesus Christ is our shepherd. He will lead us beside the quiet waters where we may quench our thirst and to those green pastures where He will guard us as we eat. He will bind up our wounds and come after us if we should wander away. He will heal our broken heart and lead us in paths of righteousness, all for the sake of His name.

Let us worship Him, our good shepherd, Jehovah-rohi!

Jehovah-Elyon

This name declares God to be the Lord Most High. There is none higher than He!

"For the Lord Most High is to be feared, a great King over all the earth."

Psalm 47:2

"For Thou art the Lord Most High over all the earth; Thou art exalted far above all gods."

Psalm 97:9

Let us worship Him, the Lord Most High, Jehovah-elyon!

Jehovah-Hoseenu

Jehovah-Hoseenu is the Lord our Maker. He is our Creator with whom we have a covenant relationship.

"Come, let us worship and bow down; Let us kneel before the Lord our Maker."

Psalm 95:6

Let us worship Him, the Lord our Maker, Jehovah-hoseenu!

Jehovah-Eloheenu

In this name God declares Himself as the Lord our God. He is both Lord *and* holy God to those who have entered into a covenant with Him.

> *"Exalt the Lord our God, and worship at His footstool;*
> *Holy is He...O Lord our God, Thou didst answer them;*
> *Thou wast a forgiving God to them, and yet an avenger*
> *of their evil deeds. Exalt the Lord our God, and worship*
> *at His holy hill, for holy is the Lord our God."*
>
> Psalm 99:5,8,9

Let us worship Him, the Lord our God, Jehovah-Eloheenu!

Jehovah-Elohim

The first of many occurrences of this title, the Lord God, is seen in the second chapter of Genesis,

> *"These are the generations of the heavens and of the earth*
> *when they were created, in the day that the Lord God*
> *made the earth and the heavens."*
>
> Genesis 2:4

This name declares the Self-Existent One, the Eternal Creator, in covenant relationship with His people. Let us worship Him, the Lord God, Jehovah-elohim!

Jehovah-Eloheka

When God gave Moses the ten commandments, He said that He was Jehovah-eloheka, Israel's Lord,

> *"I am the Lord your God, who brought you out of the land*
> *of Egypt, out of the house of slavery...You shall not*

worship them or serve them; for I, the Lord your God, am a jealous God... You shall not take the name of the Lord your God in vain...

Exodus 20:2,5,7

Worship Him, the Lord your God, Jehovah-eloheka!

Jehovah-Elohay

God revealed Himself in even more of a personal relationship with His people in general, and to the prophet Zechariah, specifically,

"...Then the Lord, my God, will come, and all the holy ones with Him! And it will come about in that day that there will be no light; the luminaries will dwindle. For it will be a unique day which is known to the Lord, neither day nor night, but it will come about that at evening time there will be light. And the Lord will be king over all the earth; in that day the Lord will be the only one, and His name the only one."

Zechariah 14:5-7,9

Let each of us worship Him, the Lord my God, Jehovah-elohay!

Jehovah-Sabaoth

Perhaps the most famous passage in the Old Testament is the story of David and Goliath. It contains further revelation of God's character as Jehovah-sabaoth, the Lord of Hosts. Here, the giant, Goliath, taunted the entire Israelite army, until finally a champion emerged, a young shepherd boy. After some consideration, David ventured forth, not with the unfamiliar weapons of the army, but with his familiar staff and sling,

"And the Philistine said to David, 'Am I a dog, that you come to me with sticks?' And the Philistine cursed David by his gods. And the Philistine also said to David, 'Come to me, and I will give your flesh to the birds of the sky

and the beasts of the field.' Then David said to the
Philistine, 'You come to me with a sword, a spear, and
a javelin, but I come to you in the name of the Lord of
Hosts (Jehovah-sabaoth), the God of the armies of Israel,
whom you have taunted.' ''

I Samuel 17:43-45

David charged and defeated the enemy of Israel because he
advanced in the name of the God he served. We, too, can defeat
every "giant" in the name of the Lord.

Let us worship Him, the Lord of hosts, Jehovah-sabaoth!

The Jehovah names were given, beginning with Abraham, to the
children of Israel. To the Gentile nations God was known as the
Eternal Creator, but not as their Lord.

When God declared that He was Jehovah (Lord) to Abraham,
a special union was formed. He was no longer a distant Creator
watching His creation from afar. From that moment on He was Lord,
Master and King who would forever be personally involved with
His subjects. As Lord He promised to protect, to guide and direct,
to provide for, and to love His people like a father for his children.
This relationship did not apply to all the inhabitants of the earth,
but only to Abraham and his descendants. The only thing God
required in return was their love and obedience.

It may appear that the promises given to the children of Israel
do not have any relevance to the Christian today. Weren't the
covenant names for Abraham and his seed only? Yes, but these
promises apply to us, too. We will see how this is possible, even
though most of us are not physically descended from Abraham.

As Christians we have been born again through faith. As it is
written in Ephesians 2:8,9,

"For by grace you have been saved through faith; and
that not of yourselves, it is the gift of God."

Ephesians 2:8,9

By faith in Jesus Christ we become recipients of a heritage given
only to the Jewish nation. How glorious is this truth!

"And the Scripture, forseeing that God would justify the Gentiles by faith, preached the gospel beforehand to Abraham, saying, 'All the nations shall be blessed in you.' So then those who are of faith are blessed with Abraham, the believer. Christ redeemed us from the curse of the Law, having become a curse for us; for it is written, 'Cursed is everyone who hangs on a tree' - in order that in Christ Jesus the blessing of Abraham might come to the Gentiles, so that we might receive the promise of the Spirit through faith. For you are all sons of God through faith in Jesus Christ. And if you belong to Christ, then you are Abraham's offspring, heirs according to promise."

Galatians 3:8-9,13-14,26-29

As we see from this Scripture, God is our Father because of all that Jesus Christ accomplished through His life, death and resurrection. Summarizing then, who is the God we worship?

He is, first of all, Elohim, the Eternal Creator who always was and always will be, and He is El Shaddai, our strength, the source of comfort, confidence and nourishment. He is Jehovah-jireh, who has seen our needs and provided for them even before we know them, and Jehovah-nissi, the One who still calls us to rally around Him so He can perform miracles on our behalf. He is Jehovah-rophe, our Great Physician, and Jehovah-shalom, our peace in every situation, regardless of how circumstances may appear. Jehovah-tsidkenu is the One who gives us His righteousness in exchange for our sins and Jehovah-m'kaddesh sanctifies us through His own precious blood. He is Jehovah-shammah who is always present with us and in us, and Jehovah-rohi, the Shepherd who leads us to quiet waters and green pastures. Jehovah-elyon is the Most High exalted above all and Jehovah-hoseenu is He who knows us even in our mother's womb. Jehovah-eloheenu is the Lord our God; Jehovah-eloheka is the Lord thy God and Jehovah-elohay is the Lord my God. Finally, He is Jehovah-sabaoth, the Lord of all the hosts of heaven and earth. This is our great and glorious God, revealed through His names.

Even though the Lord has many different facets and a name for each of His characteristics, He is still a Trinity - Father, Son and Holy Spirit. Here in the concept of the Trinity we find an antinomy. This, as we learned in our discussion of a humble heart, consists of two ideas that appear contradictory, but in reality, are both true. In the divine Trinity, there are three who are God, and yet, "the Lord our God is one."

God the Father, the first Person of the Trinity, is to be worshipped by all true believers because this is His desire,

> *"But an hour is coming, and now is, when the true worshippers shall worship the Father in spirit and truth; for such people the Father seeks to be His worshippers."*
>
> John 4:23

We worship our Father because He is the holy Father and the righteous Father (John 17:16,35). He is the Father of glory (Ephesians 1:17), and the Father of light, from whom all good things come (James 1:17). He is the Father of mercies (II Corinthians 1:3), and the Father of our Lord Jesus Christ (Ephesians 1:3, I Peter 1:3 and Timothy 3:16). Not only do we worship Him for who He is, but for what He has done. The Father, above all else, has loved us with an everlasting love,

> *"For God so loved the world, that He gave His only begotten Son, that whosoever believes in Him should not perish, but have eternal life."*
>
> John 3:16

> *"The Lord appeared to him from afar, saying, "I have loved you with an everlasting love; therefore I have drawn you with lovingkindness."*
>
> Jeremiah 31:3

He manifested this love when He sent His own Son for us (I John 1:9) that we might be sons of God (I John 3:1). By the Father of our Lord we have been blessed with all spiritual blessings, chosen in him, predestinated unto adoption, made acceptable, redeemed and forgiven, and made aware of the mystery of His will. (Ephesians

1:3-9). Finally, the Father has made it possible for us to enter into His presence to worship Him,

> *"Since therefore, brethren, we have confidence to enter the holy place by the blood of Jesus, by a new and living way which He inaugurated for us through the veil, that is, His flesh, and since we have a great priest over the house of God, let us draw near with a sincere heart in full assurance of faith, having our hearts sprinkled clean from an evil conscience and our bodies washed with pure water."*
>
> Hebrews 10:19-22

Yes, the way has been prepared for us to worship Him through the Son, our Lord and Savior. Jesus Christ, Son of the Most High, declared,

> *"I am the way, the truth and the life: no man cometh unto the Father but by me."*
>
> John 14:6

There is no way to the Father, Jehovah-God, except by receiving His Son. Jesus Christ, like the Father, is to be worshipped for who He is, for what He has done, what He is doing and for what He is yet to do. It is written in the Scriptures,

> *"In the beginning was the Word, and the Word was with God, and the Word was God. He was in the beginning with God. All things came into being by Him, and apart from Him nothing came into being that came into being. And the Word became flesh, and dwelt among us, and we beheld His glory, glory as of the only begotten from the Father, full of grace and truth."*
>
> John 1:1-3,14

> *"For by Him all things were created, both in the heavens and on earth, visible and invisible, whether thrones or dominions or rulers or authorities - all things have been*

created by Him and for Him.''

Colossians 1:16

Jesus, the Living Word, played the premier role in the creation of all things. We find also, that it is the Lord Jesus who revealed the Father to the world,

> *"No man has seen God at any time; the only begotten Son, who is in the bosom of the Father, He has explained Him.''*

John 1:18

One way in which Jesus accomplished explaining the Father to mankind was by taking on flesh and blood. A child once said that Jesus came as ''God with skin on.'' He became the fulfillment of the characteristics of God as revealed through His covenant names. In Jesus' own words,

> *"And now, glorify Thou Me together with Thyself, Father, with the glory which I had with Thee before the world was. **I manifested Thy name** to the men who Thou gavest Me out of the world; Thine they were, and Thou gavest them to Me, and they have kept Thy word.''*

John 17:5,6

Throughout the gospel of John, He declared who He was in what some have called the ''I Am revelations.'' How similar in nature they are to the covenant names of God!

> *"**I am the bread of life**; he who comes to Me shall not hunger, and he who believes in Me shall never thirst.''*

John 6:35

> *"**I am the light of the world**; he who follows Me shall not walk in the darkness, but shall have the light of life.''*

John 8:12

> *"**I am the door**; if anyone enters through Me, he shall*

be saved, and shall go in and out and find pasture.''
John 10:9

*''**I am the good shepherd**; the good shepherd lays down his life for the sheep...I am the good shepherd, and I know my own, and My own know Me.''*
John 10:11,14

*''**I am the resurrection and the life**; he who believes in Me shall live even if he dies.''*
John 11:25

*''**I am the way, the truth, and the life**; no one comes to the Father but through Me.''*
John 14:6

*''**I am the true vine**, and My Father is the vinedresser. Every branch in Me that does not bear fruit, He takes away; and every branch that bears fruit, He prunes it, that it may bear more fruit.''*
John 15:1,2

The Lord Jesus is, to all those who are His own, the embodiment of every promise inherent in the name Jehovah. God told Moses in Exodus 3:14, *''**I AM** WHO I AM.''* Jesus revealed the same thing of Himself in the New Testament. Jesus not only provided food from heaven; He is the Bread of life which came down from above. He is the true Vine who always bears healthy fruit and the good Shepherd who gave His life for the sheep. We will never walk in darkness because He is the Light that reproves all darkness. Jesus is the only way to the Father; in fact, He is the very Door through which we must enter. He died, but that was not the end. He gives us true life because He arose from the dead and lives forevermore. He doesn't *have* life...He *is* life itself!

Jesus the man was God incarnate, as was foretold by the prophet Isaiah,

''For a child will be born to us, a son will be given to

us; and the government will rest on His shoulders; and
His name will be called Wonderful Counselor, Mighty
God, Eternal Father, Prince of Peace.''

Isaiah 9:6

As the Prince of Peace, He lived a holy life in perfect obedience
to His heavenly Father, and finished the work He was given. He
was the voluntary and substitutionary sacrifice on behalf of all who
would accept Him as such. After the resurrection Jesus gloriously
ascended into heaven, where He now sits at the right hand of the
Father. There He presides as Head over the Church. At the end of
the age, He will return to fulfill His promise to His people,

"For the Lord Himself will descend from heaven with a
shout, with the voice of the archangel, and with the
trumpet of God; and the dead in Christ shall rise first.
Then we who are alive and remain shall be caught up
together with them in the clouds to meet the Lord in the
air, and thus shall we shall always be with the Lord.''

I Thessalonians 4:16,17

Hallelujah! How can we keep from responding with worship and
adoration to such a glorious God?

These passages have given us some insight into the nature of the
Father and the Son. What of the Holy Spirit, the third Person of
the Trinity? Are we to worship Him? No. We are not instructed
to worship the Holy Spirit, although He is as much God, as Father
and Son. It is the Spirit who instructs and empowers us to worship.

The Holy Spirit is the Person of the Trinity through which God
communicates with us. In the Old Testament the word, ''ruach,''
was translated into spirit two hundred thirty times. In the New
Testament, it was the word, ''pneuma.'' Both of these words have
similar meaning and imply an invisible force, akin to the breath of
God.

There is only one way to worship properly - through the leading
and power of the Holy Spirit. He is the One who guides us, through
the Word of God, to an ever-increasing appreciation of the Father
and Son. We must not rely solely on either the Scriptures or the

Spirit of God, but on a balance of each. The Holy Spirit will never lead anyone to do anything contrary to the Word of God, but will lead the believer to a deeper and fuller revelation of the Divine.

Numerous are the Christians who study the Bible, but yet are unable to see the more profound things of God. It takes the Holy Spirit to reveal them to us. We must, therefore, rely totally upon His guidance and demand that our entire being - spirit, soul and body - submit to Him. When we do this, our study and prayer times, as well as our praise and worship, will produce much spiritual fruit.

As mere human beings we do not know how to worship God. Yes, as Christians, the Holy Spirit lives within us, but we must learn to follow Him to "worship in Spirit and in truth." Many evangelical services and much "gospel music" cater only to man's emotions. Our emotional capacity is part of the soul (mind, will and emotions) and not the spirit. In order for there to be true worship, or for that matter, a genuine "new birth," our spirit must join with God's Spirit. Bob Mumford said it concisely, "When Spirit and spirit meet - there is worship!"[17]

Scripture tells us that *God is love*. The three elements that made up the love triangle (knowledge, worship and covenant) are so important because they are a shadowing of Him. Not only is our love of God comprised of these elements; God *is* the ultimate in knowledge, worship and covenant. Throughout the Bible we see God exhibiting these characteristics. For our purpose, we will limit this discussion to the verses referring to the Holy Spirit. The same principles apply to the Father and Son because they are One.

The Holy Spirit has knowledge and intelligence. We are told that He knows, speaks, intercedes, teaches, hears and guides,

> *"And in the same way the Spirit also helps our weakness;*
> *for we do not know how to pray as we should, but the*
> *Spirit Himself intercedes for us with groanings too deep*
> *for words; and He who searches the hearts knows what*
> *the mind of the Spirit is, because He intercedes for the*
> *saints according to the will of God."*
>
> Romans 8:26-27

> *"But the Helper, the Holy Spirit, whom the Father will*

send in My name, He will teach you all things, and bring
to your remembrance all that I have said to you.''

John 14:26

''But when He, the Spirit of truth comes, He will guide
you into all the truth; for He will not speak on His own
initiative, but whatever He hears, He will speak; and He
will disclose to you what is to come.''

John 16:13

The Holy Spirit has emotions and feelings also, because it was said
of Him that He was grieved, and can be quenched or despised,

''And do not grieve the Holy Spirit of God, by whom you
were sealed for the day of redemption.''

Ephesians 4:30

''Do not quench the Spirit.''

I Thessalonians 5:19

''How much severer punishment do you think he will
deserve who has trampled under foot the Son of God,
and has regarded as unclean the blood of the covenant
by which he was sanctified, and has insulted the Spirit
of grace?''

Hebrews 10:29

Finally, we see the Holy Spirit as having a will and being committed,
for He strives, reproves, and shows,

''Then the Lord said, ''My Spirit shall not strive with man
forever, because he also is flesh...''

Genesis 6:3

''For the flesh sets its desire against the Spirit, and the
Spirit against the flesh; for these are in opposition to one
another, so that you may not do the things that you
please.''

Galatians 5:17

The Holy Spirit has many titles in the Word of God, as well as many different abilities and functions. Above all, He is absolutely holy. He is the Spirit of truth and our Comforter. He is the Spirit of God, the Spirit of grace, the Spirit of Christ, the Spirit of glory, the Spirit of promise, and His mission is to glorify the Son, Jesus Christ.

During creation the Holy Spirit brooded over the waters of the chaotic earth. He inspired all Scripture (II Timothy 3:16); was present in Christ's incarnation (Luke 1:25); in Jesus' life on earth (Matthew 3:16) and in His death. It was through the eternal Spirit that He offered Himself to God (Hebrews 9:14). In Jesus' post-resurrection ministry we see that "He, through the Holy Ghost, had given commandments unto the apostles" (Acts 1:2). Everywhere, we see the Holy Spirit at work!

In the world, the Holy Spirit convicts man of his sin and of his need for a Savior. Man is made aware of his unrighteousness and his inability to meet God's requirements for holiness. Those who do accept Jesus' sacrifice as a gift are sealed with the Spirit until the day of redemption. Having the seal of the Holy Spirit assures us that God will fulfill all His promises. How does He know our every need?

> *"For the eyes of the Lord move to and fro throughout the earth that He may strongly support those whose heart is completely His..."*
>
> II Chronicles 16:9

> *"Behold, the eye of the Lord is on those who fear Him, on those who hope for His lovingkindness, to deliver their soul from death, and to keep them alive in famine."*
>
> Psalm 33:18,19

Our God is truly omniscient, omnipresent and omnipotent. He desires that we come to know the splendor of His majesty so we can worship Him freely and joyfully. For, as John Piper said, "Worship is a way of gladly reflecting back to God the radiance of His worth."[18]

(Information on the Trinity is from *Worship*, by A.P. Gibbs)[19]

Chapter 6

Of Tabernacles and Temples

No book on worship would be quite complete without looking at the setting for Old Testament worship. The precise directions for the construction of the Tabernacle in the Wilderness, given to Moses so many thousands of years ago, contain a wealth of revelation. Hidden there are secrets of God's plan for man throughout the ages. It tells how we, as temples of the living God, should conduct ourselves as worshippers. John MacArthur cautioned,

> *"Worship is not giddy. It does not rush into God's presence unprepared and insensitive to His majesty. It is not shallow, superficial, or flippant. Worship is life lived in the presence of an infinitely righteous and onmnipresent God by one utterly aware of His holiness and consequently overwhelmed with his own unholiness."*[20]

What does it mean to be "living temples?" The life-changing truths contained within the ancient tabernacle will help us to answer this question. As a base from which to start, we will describe this Old Covenant place of worship. (Each detail has special significance, so we will proceed slowly through this section).

Many of us have often missed these precious gems by assuming that the Old Testament was just an unending list of needless information. Although God's manner of dealing with man has changed from dispensation to dispensation, His principles remain unchanged by time. Let us approach the tabernacle with the attitude of one seeking buried treasure. Even the most minute details, in the way they foreshadow the Messiah, serve to confirm the perfection of God.

The tabernacle of the congregation was to be situated in a strategic way among the twelve tribes. The precise order in which they were to be arranged is recorded in Numbers 2:2,

> *"The sons of Israel shall camp, each by his own standard,*
> *with the banners of their fathers' households; they shall*
> *camp around the tent of meeting at a distance."*

The tribes of Judah, Issachar and Zebulun were to camp on the eastern side; on the south side, the tribes of Reuben, Simeon, and Gad. On the west side were to be located the tribes of Ephraim, Manasseh, and Benjamin, while Dan, Asher and Naphtali completed the arrangement on the north side. The tabernacle, then, was located at the very center of the encampment, and the sons of Aaron and the Levites, those set aside to minister to God, were the only ones to make their camp near the tabernacle.

This tribal arrangement made a dramatic statement concerning worship. It was to be at the very center of their lives. Yet, they were to make their camp "far off," and only the priests and Levites were allowed to approach. This symbolized the covenant relationship that God established with His people for that time - only those in the priesthood were able to come into God's presence. Organizing the camp in this way offered certain advantages. Everyone could see the tabernacle with an unobstructed view whenever Moses went in to meet with God,

> *"And it came about, whenever Moses entered the tent, that*
> *all the people would arise and stand, each at the entrance*
> *of his tent and gaze after Moses until he entered the tent.*
> *And it came about, whenever Moses entered the tent, the*
> *pillar of cloud would descend and stand at the entrance*
> *of the tent and the Lord would speak with Moses. When*
> *all the people saw the pillar of cloud standing at the*
> *entrance of the tent, all the people would arise and*
> *worship, each at the entrance of his tent."*
>
> Exodus 33:8-10

At any other time, all one could see while looking at the tabernacle was a white linen fence-like enclosure and the badger skin covering the roof, visible above the fence. Located on the east side of the outer enclosure was the only entrance. Over this gate were hangings of blue, purple, scarlet and white linen. Passing through the gate and entering the courtyard, one would be confronted by three distinct objects: the laver, the brazen altar and the tabernacle itself. Under Mosaic law, only those chosen to minister to the Lord could actually enter the house of God. Before doing so, they first had to be cleansed in the laver, which was a large brass basin located just outside the door of the tabernacle,

> *"And Aaron and his sons shall wash their hands and their feet from it; when they enter the tent of meeting, they shall wash with water, that they may not die; or when they approach the altar to minister, by offering up in smoke a fire sacrifice to the Lord. So they shall wash their hands and their feet, that they may not die; and it shall be a perpetual statute for them, for Aaron, and his descendants throughout their generations."*
>
> Exodus 30:19-21

Adjacent to the laver was the brazen altar. As we just read, the priests had to be clean before they could offer a sacrifice. The penalty for failing to obey was death. Then, it was an actual physical death and now, it is more of a spiritual death. Both the altar and the laver were constructed of brass, the laver solid, while the altar was made of shittim wood overlaid with brass.

The roof of the tabernacle was a four-layered tent. Its inner-most layer consisted of curtains of fine white linen, blue, purple and scarlet. Covering this multicolored fabric were eleven curtains of goats' hair. The next layer was a covering of rams' skins dyed red and finally, the outer covering was of badger skins. Boards of shittim wood, overlaid with gold on the side facing inward, made up the walls of the tabernacle. The door was made of hangings of white, blue, purple and scarlet, supported by five shittim wood posts overlaid with gold on a base of brass.

Just inside the tabernacle in the holy place, there were three objects: one directly ahead, one to the left and one to the right. On the left stood a candlestick that was made of one solid piece of beaten gold, from which came all the light in the holy place,

> *"Then you shall make a lampstand of pure gold. The lampstand and its base and its shaft are to be made of hammered work; its cups, its bulb and its flowers shall be of one piece with it. And six branches shall go out from its sides, three branches of the lampstand from its one side, and three branches of the lampstand from its other side. Then you shall make its lamps seven in number, and they shall mount its lamps so as to shed light on the space in front of it."*
>
> Exodus 25:31-32,37

The second object, on the right side of the room, was the table of showbread constructed of shittim wood overlaid with pure gold. The priests kept bread on it continually before the Lord. The third and final object in the holy place was the altar of incense, again of shittim wood covered with pure gold. On this altar was burned the holy incense each morning so that there would be a never-ending sweet smell before the Lord.

Directly behind the altar of incense was a veil that separated the holy place from the most holy place (holy of holies), where the ark of the covenant was kept. This veil was made of the same four colors: blue, purple, scarlet and white linen. In the most holy place was one object only, the ark. This ark, or chest, was constructed again of shittim wood covered both inside and out with pure gold. On top of the ark was the mercy seat made of one solid piece of pure gold. Two cherubim with their wings outstretched and their faces looking toward one another stood on the mercy seat.

Such was the tabernacle that God directed the children of Israel to build for a meeting place with Him. The symbolism throughout is rich. Let us now take a closer look.

Each of the four colors in the curtains and wall hangings pointed toward specific aspects of the character and work of Jesus. The first color was white, symbolic of Jesus as the God-man and spoke of the perfect life He lived while on earth. Blue declared Jesus as the

High Priest and purple testified of His Kingship. Finally, scarlet revealed our Lord as the Suffering Savior.

From this starting point, can we see why the outer enclosure leading to the courtyard was made only of white linen? When we look at the life of Jesus we see him first in light of His perfect, yet human life. His absolute purity set Him apart from everyone else. We may not realize, from a casual glance, that He was and is Emmanuel, God with us. Purity and holiness should characterize the lifestyle (outer enclosure) of every worshipper. As with the tabernacle, this is all others see. The Holy Spirit will use the purity of our lives to inspire them to want to know more about Jesus.

For the person drawn closer to the tabernacle, there stood a solitary gate with hangings of all four colors. This gate represented the Lord Jesus as the only way into God's presence. We are reminded that He declared Himself to be the Way, the Truth, and the Life, in addition to being the Door of the sheepfold. It is through this gate that we pass when we accept Him as our Savior and are born-again. We should overflow with joy because we have been saved and can enter the presence of God. This joy is one of seven keys found in Psalm 100 that will greatly enhance our life of worship.

> *"Shout joyfully to the Lord, all the earth.*
> *Serve the Lord with gladness.*
> *Come before Him with joyful singing.*
> *Know that the Lord Himself is God.*
> *It is He who has made us, and not we ourselves;*
> *We are His people and the sheep of His pasture.*
> **Enter His gates with thanksgiving, and His courts with**
> **praise.**
> *Give thanks to Him; bless His name.*
> *For the Lord is good; His lovingkindness is everlasting,*
> *And His faithfulness to all generations."*

The first two commands should characterize our walk with the Lord - to let our joy and willingness to serve God be seen by all the world. The third command is to sing as we come before the Lord. The Israelites did this as they went to the tabernacle, and later in Scripture, to the temple in Jerusalem. Along the way they praised

God on instruments and with uplifted voices to prepare for a meeting with Him.

Once at the place of worship, the next two commands come into play. The first is that we must know who it is we worship: Father, Son and Holy Spirit in all their wondrous glory. He is our Maker; we are His. Next, the psalmist urges us again to come singing our thanks and praise. The sixth command is to be thankful for having been in the presence of our God and the seventh is to bless His name because of His great goodness.

These seven commands, or keys, are as applicable today as they ever were, even more so now that *we* have become living temples. At the moment we accept Jesus as our Lord and Savior, we pass from death to life. In one respect, we then begin living in the outer enclosure, or the court. However, many Christians remain there for the rest of their lives. They are satisfied merely with their salvation and fail to pursue God ferevently enough to enter the holy place and ultimately, the holy of holies.

Since we have even been able to enter the courtyard, our hearts should always be full of jubilant praise and thanksgiving. These will lead us on to the lifestyle of true worship we desire. Praise is such an important facet of worship, that we will we include one more song by the "sweet psalmist of Israel." Psalm 150 begins and ends with the command to praise, and in between, tells us where, why, how and who should praise the Lord,

> "Praise the Lord!
> Praise God in His sanctuary;
> Praise Him in His mighty expanse.
> Praise Him for His mighty deeds;
> Praise Him according to His excellent greatness.
> Praise Him with trumpet sound;
> Praise Him with harp and lyre;
> Praise Him with timbrel and dancing;
> Praise Him with stringed instruments and pipe.
> Praise Him with loud cymbals;
> Praise Him with resounding cymbals;
> Let everything that has breath praise the Lord.
> Praise the Lord!"

Having entered the gate, the next stop was the laver. This basin, as we mentioned, was made of highly polished brass, so that when the priests washed their hands and feet, they saw their faces reflected in it,

> *"And he made the laver of brass, and the foot of it brass,*
> *from the mirrors of the serving women who served the*
> *doorway of the tent of meeting."*
>
> Exodus 38:8

The laver is a symbol of the Word of God, referred to as a mirror in the book of James,

> *"For if anyone is a hearer of the word and not a doer, he*
> *is like a man who looks at his natural face in a mirror."*
>
> James 1:23

This laver had a dual purpose. According to Judson Cornwall, it "offered a place of both self-inspection and self-purification, for the same basin that revealed defilement afforded the means to remove that contamination."[21] From the book of Ephesians we find that we are to apply the Word to accomplish the washing, as the priests washed themselves in the laver,

> *"...that He might sanctify her, having cleansed her by the*
> *washing of water with the Word, that He might present*
> *to Himself the church in all her glory, having no spot*
> *or wrinkle or any such thing; but that she should be holy*
> *and blameless."*
>
> Ephesians 5:26,27

It is through the daily application of the Word of God to our lives that we are cleansed from the ways of the world. As we diligently wash ourselves, we will be led to the next step, the brazen altar. The significance of the sacrificial altar can only be found in the Word, which is why the laver was the first step. On the altar there were to be continual burnt offerings, morning and evening. These offerings foreshadowed Jesus Christ, The Lamb of God. They are also symbolic of God's requirements in each of our lives. A further study of the offerings and sacrifices will give much useful insight as to what Jesus accomplished on the cross and God's provision for our entering His presence in worship.

There were five separate offerings described in the book of Leviticus. The following summary will provide a key to the meaning of each:

> *"Burnt offering*   **Surrender** *of Christ for the world*
> *Meal offering*   **Service** *of Christ in life*
> *Peace offering*   **Serenity** *of Christ in life*
> *Sin offering*   **Substitute** *of Christ for sin*
> *Trespass offering* **Satisfaction** of Christ for demands of
> God"*[22]

The first offering was the burnt, or ascending offering that symbolized Jesus' willingness to be the perfect sacrificial Lamb for the redemption of a lost world. In it, we also see the necessity of our acceptance of this act of love and a total consecration of our lives to Him. Our surrender is to be as voluntary as our Lord's - we surrender to Him at the moment of salvation and every day thereafter for the rest of our lives. We cannot become worshippers until we have uncompromisingly dedicated ourselves to Him.

In the Old Testament, every sacrificial animal was to be killed, its blood sprinkled on and about the altar and then totally consumed by fire, "a burnt sacrifice, an offering made by fire, of a sweet savor unto the Lord" (Leviticus 1:17). This shedding and sprinkling of blood was a foreshadowing of the crucifixion and the power of the Lamb's blood as the only means of cleansing from sin. Likewise, each of us must be spiritually cleansed with Jesus' blood. As the offering on the brazen altar was consumed by fire, so must our hearts be passionately on fire with love for God.

The meal (grain) offering was symbolic of the manner in which Christ gave Himself to the Father for the service of man. This can be seen in the description of the offering,

> *"Now when anyone presents a grain offering as an offering*
> *to the Lord, his offering shall be of fine flour, and he*
> *shall pour oil on it and put frankincense on it...and the*

*priest shall offer it up in smoke as its memorial portion
on the altar, an offering by fire of a soothing aroma to
the Lord.''*

Leviticus 2:1,2

Here, the use of fine flour symbolized Jesus as the Bread of Life,
untainted with sin, who had the fullness of the Holy Spirit (oil) poured
out upon Him. Frankincense had a bitter taste when eaten, but a
beautiful scent when burned. This was prophetic, giving us insight
into the bitter agony and humiliation that Jesus would endure, as
well as how pleasing His uncompromising obedience would be to
the Father.

The fourth offering was performed every time someone broke
one of God's laws, and was symbolic of Jesus' substitutionary
sacrifice for the sins of mankind,

*''...if a person sins unintentionally in any of the things
which the Lord has commanded not to be done, and
commits any of them, if the anointed priest sins so as
to bring guilt on the people, then let him offer to the
Lord...''*

Leviticus 4:2,3

The animal was killed in the same manner as the other offerings,
but the blood was sprinkled in a different and specific way,
symbolizing the strong power inherent in the shed blood of Jesus
to open the way for all believers to enter God's presence,

*''and the priest shall dip his finger in the blood, and
sprinkle some of the blood seven times before the Lord,
in front of the veil of the sanctuary.''*

Leviticus 4:6

The fifth offering was the trespass (guilt) offering and this covered
any sin against the Lord's holy things. In addition to the animal
sacrifice, there was to be a sum of money paid to the one who was
offended or injured,

"If a person acts unfaithfully and sins unintentionally
against the Lord's holy things, then he shall bring his
guilt offering to the Lord; a ram without defect from the
flock, according to your valuation in silver by shekels,
in terms of the shekel of the sanctuary, for a guilt offering,
and it shall be forgiven him.''

Leviticus 5:15

All of these offerings should lead us to a fuller appreciation of the costliness of sin and the tremendous penalty already paid on our behalf by the Son of God. Sin bears a heavy price! Never again should we take sin, no matter how slight we think it may be, as a light matter. It cost Jesus His very life.

These offerings were very much a part of the everyday life of all Old Testament Jews. The animal sacrifices and offerings have passed away, but the principle behind them has not. Our own worship and offerings should cost us something. If they don't, are they really true sacrifices? This is not to say we must pay or work in order for our sins to be forgiven. Jesus fulfilled this requirement once and for all by giving His life on the Cross. It is only through the blood of Jesus (brazen altar), as it is revealed through the Word (laver), that we have access to the presence of God. If we are to follow in His footsteps, we must, of our own free will, pick up *our* cross and give our lives as an offering. Every fleshly desire must be crucified,

"I urge you therefore, brethren, by the mercies of God,
to present your bodies a living and holy sacrifice,
acceptable to God, which is your spiritual service of
worship.''

Romans 12:1

At this point, one would be standing outside the door of the tabernacle itself. Before entering within, let us look at what the outside of the tabernacle had to say. The curtains of four colors once again foretold of Jesus in all His glory: Perfect Man, Priest, King and Savior. Covering the beautiful, colored curtains were more curtains of woven goats' hair. As one could imagine, they would be roughly textured even after being woven together. This was symbolic of the life of Jesus. His wasn't the polished life of the kingly courts, but the rough existence of a carpenter and traveling preacher.

In the rams' skins dyed red, there was the revelation of Jesus as the sacrificial Lamb, and the badgers' skins as the outer covering pointed towards His portrait that would be painted by the words of the prophet Isaiah,

> *"For He grew up before Him like a tender shoot, and like a root out of parched ground; He had no stately form or majesty that we should look upon Him, nor appearance that we should be attracted to Him. He was despised and forsaken of men, a man of sorrows, and acquainted with grief; and like one from whom men hide their face, He was despised, and we did not esteem Him."*
>
> Isaiah 53:2,3

After Jesus was beaten, scourged and hung on a cross to die, His outward appearance was horrifying to behold. The truth of who He really was remained hidden. Similarly, the glory of the presence of God within the tabernacle was completely hidden from view by the ugly animal skins covering it. Thus far, we have met Jesus as the Perfect Man (outer enclosure), the Suffering Savior and been introduced to Him as the great High Priest (brazen altar). If we are to come to know intimately our High Priest and King, we must take the next step.

The door of the tabernacle was different from that of the outer enclosure, in that it was supported by five posts instead of four. These posts symbolize the five-fold ministry that began with the infilling of the Holy Spirit on the day of Pentecost. The ministries of the apostle, prophet, evangelist, pastor and teacher lead us through the door and on to a deeper revelation of Jesus. Pure gold covered the five posts, speaking of the purity that must be present in their lives. The brass bases indicate that they must be tried by fire and suffering before they can lead. These ministries, then, after they have been proven and anointed by God, are able to bring the people into His holy presence.

Once inside the holy place one was confronted with an awesome sight - wall to wall gold. This revealed the absolute purity of Jesus, as well the need for purity in the life of one who would worship. Here in the holy place there was one object that gave light, the golden lampstand with its seven lamps. The source of light, the lampstand, symbolized our Lord, as He had been anointed with the fullness of the Holy Spirit, and the lamps represented the seven spirits,

> *"And the spirit of the Lord will rest on Him, the spirit of wisdom and understanding, the spirit of counsel and strength, the spirit of knowledge and the fear of the Lord."*
>
> Isaiah 11:2

The lampstand was hammered into the proper shape from one piece of gold, and only pure, beaten olive oil could be burned in it. Every morning and evening the priests cleaned and trimmed the lamps' wicks and added fresh oil to insure that the light would burn continually.

In this description, we find some clues that tell us how to become better vessels of the Spirit of God. Both the candlestick and the olive oil had to be beaten before the light could shine. We must allow God to have His way in us, just as our Lord suffered Himself to be beaten for our transgressions. Jesus is the Light and He became the "Light of the world" (John 9:5), by obediently submitting to the Father.

There is something else of which we should take note. Once we have voluntarily placed ourselves on the altar of sacrifice and consecrated our lives to God, He is the One who must be in complete control. He is the "Boss." Through the anointed ministry of the church, God shows us the way to the holy place. Once inside, He leads us by the Light of the world, the Spirit of our Lord. The Spirit alone can guide us into the presence of God; we simply submit to His leading.

Directly across from the lampstand in the holy place was the table of showbread. This foreshadowed the Lord Jesus as the Bread of Life, whose body was broken for the world. The celebration of Holy Communion reminds us of His act of love. If we eat of the Bread, we will have eternal life,

> *"As the living Father sent Me, and I live because of the Father, so he who eats Me, he also shall live because of Me. This is the bread which came down out of heaven; not as the fathers ate, and died, he who eats this bread shall live forever."*
>
> John 6:57,58

The light from the lampstand illuminated the table of showbread in the holy place, just as the light of the Holy Spirit empowers the bread of the Word. Whether heard in an anointed sermon during a worship service, or in our personal devotions, it is the Spirit-anointed Word that sustains us.

The third object in the holy place was the golden altar of incense, located directly before the veil that separated the holy place from the most holy place. Every morning and evening as the priests filled the lamps with oil, they burned incense upon this altar. For those who desire to be true worshippers of the Lord and to come into presence, this step is of the utmost importance.

Once again, the pure gold altar signifies God's requirement for purity and holiness,

> *"Thine eyes are too pure to approve evil, and Thou canst not look on wickedness with favor..."*
>
> Habakkuk 1:13

From this we learn that, before the incense could become a sweet-smelling aroma, it had to be placed upon a pure base. So must it be in our lives; the incense of our worship to God must spring from a pure heart.

The incense is indicative of the costliness of worshipping "in the beauty of holiness" (Psalm 96:9). It was carefully prepared for use solely in the tabernacle. Three spices - stacte, onycha and galbanum were combined in equal measure with frankincense and then tempered together by heating. After it was evenly blended, it was beaten into pieces suitable for burning before the Lord. Finally, only as it was consumed by fire, did the incense release its heavenly scent. For our lives to be pleasing in God's eyes, we must also, as did our Lord Jesus, undergo the same preparation.

According to A.P. Gibbs, a worshipper's heart is composed of four parts that directly correlate to the four ingredients of the incense. The first heart ingredient is remembrance, and the focus of this should be the Person and works of Jesus Christ. Gratitude is the second element of a worshipper's heart; reverence is the third and amazement (awe), in contemplating the majesty of God's divine nature, is the fourth. These four parts must undergo the same gentle tempering process as the incense; too little or too much heat will destroy rather than blend together. The Holy Spirit, though, knows the exact temperature required to remove all the impurities from every believer.

After the Lord perfectly tempers our heart, we are ready to begin the next step. This process is by no means an easy experience. Whereas the heating may have been a bit unpleasant, this may be exceedingly painful. We should consider that if it was not an easy task for the Lord we have no right to expect to be an exception. Let us willingly submit.

After tempering, the incense was beaten into small pieces before it could be burned. In the Hebrew language the word translated "beaten" can be most accurately expressed as "crushed" or "pulverized." The same applies to us. In which part of our being, though, does the crushing take place? Our body has already been placed as a living sacrifice upon the altar of burnt offering. It is our soulish, or carnal nature, made up of our mind, will and emotions that undergoes this process. Our every desire must conform to God's purpose for us. As it is written,

> "The sacrifices of God are a broken spirit; a broken and
> a contrite heart, O God, Thou wilt not despise."
>
> Psalm 51:17

The crushing process is not a pleasant experience, but the result is worth any temporary pain. Our worship will be a pleasing aroma to the Father. He accomplishes this by fire in the same way that the priests lit the incense. First our body, then our soul and finally our spirit is consecrated to God. It is in the divine fire that we offer our spirit back to Him. The Lord Jesus underwent such a sacrifice during His agony on the cross, as evidenced by His last words,

*"And Jesus, crying out with a loud voice, said, 'Father,
into Thy hands I commit My spirit,' And having said
this, He breathed His last."*

Luke 23:46

When we, like Jesus, place our spirit into the hands of the Father,
allowing it to be totally consumed by the fire of the Holy Spirit,
then and only then are we prepared to enter into His presence. The
perfumed smoke from the burning incense rose toward the four-
colored ceiling of the ancient tabernacle. So our gaze, no longer
looking straight ahead, is fixed heavenward on the Lord in all His
glory - Perfect Man, Suffering Savior, Great High Priest and King
of Kings.

The three objects in the holy place (golden lampstand, table of
showbread and golden altar of incense) form the points of an
imaginary triangle. There is much significance in the way this relates
to the love of God triangle we studied earlier (knowledge, covenant
and worship).

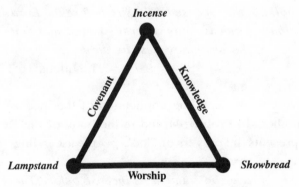

From the illustration we see that each of the points reflects to the
opposite side. It is by the light of the Holy Spirit (lampstand) that
we grow in intimate **knowledge** of our Lord. As we eat the bread
of the Word (table of showbread) our **covenant** with Him deepens.
The final fiery sacrifice of our whole being (altar of incense) releases
the sweet fragrance of our **worship**.

When we have come to **know** God intimately through Jesus Christ
and have entered into a committed **covenant** with Him, when our
spirit has been completely consumed by the fire of **worship**, then

He will lead us through the veil into the most holy place.

Earlier we read that our Lord paved the way for us to pass through the veil and come before the Father to worship at His footstool. Now, because we have followed in the Lord's steps and have been prepared by the Spirit, we are ready to commune with God. Our great High Priest takes us into the presence of Almighty God, much like the high priest entered the most holy place to stand before the ark.

Under the old covenant, only the high priest was allowed to enter the most holy place, and even then, but once a year to make atonement for the sins of the children of Israel. When he did this he had to observe every command and regulation detailing these acts. Any breach whatsoever would cost the priest his very life. One of God's directives was that he should bring incense with him and place it before the mercy seat,

> *"And he shall take a firepan full of coals of fire from upon the altar before the Lord, and two handfuls of finely ground sweet incense and bring it inside the veil. And he shall put the incense on the fire before the Lord, that the cloud of incense may cover the mercy seat that is on the ark of the testimony, lest he die."*
>
> Leviticus 16:12,13

We have already seen one implication of the incense and now we find another. In Psalm 141 and in the book of the Revelation, incense represents the prayers of God's people ascending to heaven,

> *"May my prayer be counted as incense before Thee; the lifting up of my hands as the evening offering."*
>
> Psalm 141:2

> *"And when He had taken the book, the four living creatures and the twenty-four elders fell down before the Lamb, having each one a harp, and golden bowls, full of incense, which are the prayers of the saints."*
>
> Revelation 5:8

The sole object in the most holy place was the ark of the covenant, upon which was the mercy seat and inward-looking cherubim. Not even a light detracted from the glory of the Lord. The most outstanding feature of the ark was the two cherubim who, with outstretched wings, stood as silent witnesses of God's glory. This mercy seat was to remind us that it is only through the mercy of God that He has made a way for us to come before Him and commune with Him.

> *"And there I will meet with you; and from above the mercy seat, from between the two cherubim which are upon the ark of the testimony, I will speak to you about all that I will give you in commandment for the sons of Israel."*
>
> Exodus 25:22

The ark contained the stone tablets upon which the ten commandments were written, the pot of manna and the rod of Aaron. These objects bore witness to God's miracles and foreshadowed a new covenant in Jesus.

The stone tablets were indicative of the inflexible law that God gave Moses and of the manner in which He dealt with man in the Old Testament. In the manna was a reference to Jesus as the Bread of Life. What do we find in the rod of Aaron that speaks of our Lord?

First of all, the rod was used as a means of verifying the call of Aaron and his descendants to the priesthood. God's choice was confirmed when life sprang forth out of a dead branch. This again prophesied of Jesus as the great High Priest who would miraculously be raised from the dead, and as the One who would bring new spiritual life to those who had been dead in their trespasses and sins. Even further, the rod spoke of the restoration of the twelve tribes of Israel that will occur during the great tribulation. Although the Israelites suffered spiritual death when they rejected Jesus, they will not remain there forever. New life will spring forth from that which is now dead.

Each of these truths contained within the ark make manifest one important fact: God's plan and purpose for man has always been to have fellowship with him. All that Satan stole from Adam, Jesus restored for both the Jews and the gentiles, now and forever. This is our God who from the beginning has called us to come before

Him in passionate worship.

The entire tabernacle illustrated the full scope of God's dealings with man through the ages and foretold of the coming of Jesus Christ. In Him, old and new come together to complete the restoration of our relationship with God. As true worshippers, we are called to come apart and be separate from the world rather than being caught up in its hustle and bustle. Our lives should exemplify the transformation that occurs as God's love fills us. Even at first glance, this should be readily apparent. The evidence of our being the "temple of the Holy Spirit" should be as visible as was the tabernacle of ancient days. After all, the tabernacle was one of witness, was it not?

Chapter 7

Prayer:
The Heartbeat of Worship

Prayer cannot be successfully separated from worship, for it prepares the soul for worship, expresses the spirit in worship and interacts with God, which is worship.

Worship without prayer is like daytime without light, a school without students, a choir without music, or an automobile without fuel...

The praying saint cannot keep from worshipping; the prayerless saint cannot rise to worship.*"*[23]

"Prayer is the mold in which the character of our life is shaped."*[24]

"Prayer is the sap of the vineyard. When it flows, life will manifest itself, but when it ceases to flow, the leaves brown and fall off, the fruit withers on the vine, and the plant goes into the dormant stage. Prayer is therefore not elective but essential: no prayer - no life flow; no life flow - no fruit."*[25]

*"Prayer **must** have priority. Prayer **must** be our bolt to lock up the night, our key to open the day.*"*[26]

Earlier, the act of worship was defined as practicing the presence of God and maintaining communion with Him. Only as we dedicate ourselves continually to prayer can we hope to approach a lifestyle of worship. In Paul the apostle's letter to the church at Colossae, he wrote,

79

> *"**Devote** yourselves to prayer, keeping alert in it with an attitude of thanksgiving."*
>
> Colossians 4:2

During the Lord's time of trial in the garden of Gethsemane, He directed the disciples to pray, but instead they all fell asleep,

> *"...So, you men could not keep watch with Me for one hour? Keep watching and praying, that you may not enter into temptation; the spirit is willing, but the flesh is weak."*
>
> Matthew 26:40-41

As strong as our human spirit may be, as long as we are housed in earthly temples, the weaknesses of the flesh must be overcome. Watchful prayer is one of the ways in which this is accomplished. The disciples failed to pray and we know what happened to them. They were all scattered and Peter went even so far as to deny the Lord, not once, but three times. As worshippers it is essential that we learn to be prayer warriors. We cannot expect to "sleep," as Jesus called it, all week long, and then go to church on Sunday to find the presence of God. We must commune with Him every day in our heart.

There are at least three very good reasons why we should pray. The first and foremost is that it brings honor to God. "Prayer is an act of worship, a paying homage" to our Father in heaven, as shared by A.W. Pink.[27]

The second very important reason is that prayer develops humility by bringing us to the point of total dependency upon God. Continuing in prayer will lead us to the realization that, without God, we can do nothing of lasting value. Paul summed up this thought in his letter to the Roman church when he wrote,

> *"For I know that nothing good dwells in me, that is, in my flesh; for the wishing is present in me, but the doing of good is not."*
>
> Romans 7:18

Paul knew how dependent he was upon God; so too, will every true worshipper come to discover as he learns to pray.

The third reason for praying is that we might have those things that we ask of God, for the Lord Himself, declares,

> *"Ask, and it shall be given you; seek and you shall find; knock, and it shall be opened to you. For everyone who asks receives, and he who seeks, finds, and to him who knocks it shall be opened."*
>
> Matthew 7:7,8

Yet, this is not to say that *everything* we ask of God He will give to us. He will give us those things which are in accordance with the character of our Lord. Therefore, when we petition the Father in the name of Jesus, what we should actually be doing is praying for those same things that He desires to give us, as put forth in His Word. We could say, in a sense, that we are "praying for God." Granted, this may sound a bit unorthodox at first, but it is the essence of true prayer. Our prayers should be directed towards God and the accomplishing of His purposes in the world. How often do we find our prayer time all but consumed with concerns for family, friends and finances? We should, instead, be praying for God to be glorified in every area of our lives.

Along with our personal needs, prayers should be made for our leaders, both among God's people and in the world. They should be intercessory in nature, praying that the leaders would be open to His direction, and that His kingdom would be established everywhere,

> *"First of all, then, I urge that entreaties and prayers, petitions and thanksgivings, be made on behalf of all men. For kings and all who are in authority, in order that we may lead a tranquil and quiet life in all godliness and dignity."*
>
> I Timothy 2:1,2

Let us learn to pray that God would show Himself strong on behalf of His people and that He alone would reign supreme in the kingdom of our heart. There was a man, George Mueller, who dedicated his life to helping orphaned children in England. Knowing that God had called him to that particular ministry, he depended entirely upon His support. He relied constantly on prayer and developed the following daily prayer vigil.

Each day he would expectantly read his Bible until he came upon something especially meaningful. He always read believing that God would give Him a specific word for the day, and when He did, George would write down what it meant to him. Having done this, he would meditate upon the significance of the Scriptures and examine his thoughts, allowing the Holy Spirit to bring His ultimate purpose into focus. Finally, he would speak to someone about what had been revealed to him and how it related to his life.

During his lifetime, George Mueller became accustomed to starting each day in this way and we should, if we haven't already, consider developing a similar base from which to live. (We will expound upon this idea in the following section *"Day by Day, a Lifestyle of Worship"*). True, worshipful prayer goes beyond a mere morning routine. As the day progresses we should be constantly open to have the Lord direct our every step. We must continue to watch and pray so that we can hear His voice clearly.

God has given each of us the Holy Spirit and our prayers should be a representation of that Spirit within. It is during times of prayer that we, like George Mueller, receive guidance and direction that will keep us firmly in the center of God's will. Sincere prayer, based upon God's Word and led by His Spirit, also builds character in us.

Another praying saint, Thomas Aquinas, noted that persistence in prayer consisted not of asking for many things, but of desiring *one thing*. This steadfastness will effect changes in every parameter of our existence by bringing order into a once-fragmented life. God, who is the author of order, desires that we choose this way of single-mindedness in prayer and worship.

The demand of prayer is unbelievable. In it we find that a stage will be reached where we must choose to venture forth into previously uncharted territory. We must open our heart and allow it to be developed in ways far beyond anything we, on our own, have ever attempted. True worshipful prayer involves surpassing the structure of present behavior patterns, of church traditions, and of even the rigidity of our very life in order to experience the holy and compassionate heart of the Lord. As C.H. Spurgeon once asked,

> *"Why is it that some people are often in a place of worship*
> *and yet they're not holy? It is because they neglect their*
> *(prayer) closets. They love the wheat but they do not grind*
> *it; they would have the corn but they will not go forth*
> *into the field to gather it; the fruit hangs on the tree but*
> *they will not pluck it; and the water flows at their feet*
> *but they'll not stoop to drink it."*   (Source Unknown)

Truly, achieving union and communion with the God of the universe is the essence of worship and cannot be hurried, much less neglected.

How often in our daily routine do we find ourselves so caught up in the affairs of living that we squeeze in only a few quick moments to pray? We must learn, instead, to be involved with all of our abilities to the degree in which they are enjoyable and no more. When we can pray and work, or pray and participate in sports, or pray and make love, all at a pleasant pace, life is great.

Those hurried times when we are too busy to pray, it seems as if the wheel comes off, and life is no longer a pleasant experience. A lifestyle of worship prevents us from becoming entangled in the endless merry-go-round of responsibilities. We are to be diligent, yes. However, we must not become another "Martha" who, although performing important tasks, failed to experience the most important of all. Her worldly industriousness kept her from sitting calming at the feet of the Master, basking in His love.

When studying the slow, meditative lifestyles of true worshippers, it is found that they take the time to live close to God, and to listen for rhema (specific word) from Him. They have learned how to, "be still and know that He is God" (Psalm 46:10). John Wesley, a great man of God, described how he was able to achieve this, "Though I am always in haste, I am never in a hurry because I never undertake more work than I can go through with calmness of spirit." Such calmness is developed in proportion to our growth as a worshipper whose strength is in the Lord.

How do we continue in prayer, or, as the Scriptures dictate, "pray without ceasing" (I Thessalonians 5:17)? We must maintain that right standing we have received through the blood of Jesus. The lifestyle of worship is a life of forgiving, even as the Lord Jesus forgives us, unconditionally. There can be no unconfessed sin in our lives and absolutely no unforgiveness. Every offense against us, whether real or imagined, must be forgiven even as it occurs. In His sermon on the mount, Jesus told His followers,

> *"But I say to you, love your enemies, and pray for those who persecute you."*
>
> Matthew 5:44

In praying, we should constantly examine our motives to insure that they are not selfish or out of line with God's Word. Our prayers should, as much as possible, be based upon what God has already promised. A.W. Pink, in his lecture on the Scriptures and prayer, wrote,

> *"The promises of God contain the matter of prayer and define the measure of it...Hence, the better we are acquainted with the Divine promises, and the more we are enabled to understand the goodness, grace and mercy prepared and proposed in them, the better equipped we are for acceptable prayer."*[28]

Our prayers must be acceptable to God if we expect them to be answered. We can be assured that they are by praying God's promises. Would we like to be a success in the eyes of Almighty God? For all who answer "yes," God's prescribed formula was given to Joshua as he was preparing to lead the Israelites into the Promised Land,

> *"This book of the law shall not depart from your mouth, but you shall **meditate** on it day and night, so that you may be careful to do according to all that is written in it; for then you will make your way prosperous, and then you will have success."*
>
> Joshua 1:8

From this one verse we find that, along with Joshua, we are commanded to learn the Word of God, meditate upon it continuously and declare it with our mouths to receive God's blessings. We will be able to pray with the great expectation of His power being demonstrated in, through and for us. It is not enough that we merely mouth words, putting on the appearance of holiness with no inner transformation taking place. God is aware of the desires of our heart and He requires us to hunger after His presence (Jeremiah 29:13).

The following poem was taught to A.W. Pink by his mother. How well these few simple lines express this thought,

> *"I often say my prayers,*
> *But do I ever pray?*
> *And do the wishes of my heart*
> *Go with the words I say?*
> *I may as well kneel down*
> *And worship gods of stone,*
> *As offer to the living God*
> *A prayer of words alone."* [29]

"A life formed by prayer is a life opposed to illusion, self-deception, and hypocrisy...prayer is at war with falsehood."[30] These inward attitudes are so important to our ability to worship. Time after time in the Scriptures, we find our Lord being confronted with the pious appearances of the Pharisees. In the twenty-third chapter of Matthew, is His declaration to them,

> *"Woe to you, scribes and Pharisees, hypocrites! For you*
> *clean the outside of the cup and of the dish, but inside*
> *they are full of robbery and self-indulgence. You blind*
> *Pharisees, first clean the inside of the cup and of the dish,*
> *so that the outside of it may become clean also. For you*
> *are like whitewashed tombs which on the outside appear*
> *beautiful, but inside they are full of dead men's bones*
> *and all uncleanness. Even so you too outwardly appear*
> *righteous to men, but inwardly you are full of hypocrisy*
> *and lawlessness."*
>
> Matthew 23:25-28

These are certainly not words of blessing to whom they apply, serving only to emphasize the Lord's concern over the condition of our heart. Our Father desires that we have in us the heart of Jesus and that our entire being be filled with His loving obedience. We find in the book of Hosea a brief synopsis of God's priorities,

"For I delight in loyalty rather than sacrifice, and in the knowledge of God rather than burnt offerings."

Hosea 6:6

What does all this mean for us today? Although we may not consider ourselves in the same category as the Pharisees, we are, nevertheless, in need of cleansing. The temple in Jerusalem was meant to be a house of prayer (Luke 19:46) and so are we, who have become living temples. Just as Jesus cleansed the earthly Hebrew temple, so His desire is to purge us through prayer. If we allow Him, He will accomplish this in each one of us. When our "house" becomes such a cleansed and praying vessel, we can come into the conscious presence of God...to behold the glorious light of His countenance...and commune with Him at the mercy seat. Such joy and peace experienced there is just a taste of all that awaits us in everlasting glory with Him.

Part III

ALL-CONSUMING FIRE

Chapter 8

Day by Day,
a Lifestyle of Worship

As we come to know God and trust in His Word, it is only natural that we desire to respond in a celebration of fascination, admiration, adoration, veneration, and communion. There are many ways this response is demonstrated, most of which we have mentioned at various times throughout our text. As authors Allen & Borror remind us,

> *"We are not simply spirit beings. We are more than hearts or souls or 'inner beings'. We are persons possessing an intricate complex of physical and spiritual realities. **We who worship God truly with the heart do so with our physical bodies as well.**"*[31]

Judson Cornwall, after speaking at a convention, led the people into a wonderful time of praise and worship. During this experience, the Lord spoke to him to take note of what the people were doing as they rejoiced in His presence. Some stood, some danced, some sang, each worshipping in his own way. Without any human direction, the scene changed. Some who stood lay prostrate before the Lord and some who danced then knelt and wept. All followed the leading of God in their hearts. As he watched this taking place, he heard the Lord saying to him,

> *"The lesson I want you to learn is not to make people specialists in the expression of their worship. Allow for variety both corporately and*

*individually. No one action can express all emotions, so
allow for multiple actions in each person so that his or
her worship can be complete.''*[32]

For easy reference let us now briefly summarize these avenues
of expressing, in praise and worship, our love of God.

Voice:

"I will **bless** the Lord at all times; His praise shall
continually be in my **mouth**."

Psalm 34:1

*"Be glad in the Lord and rejoice you righteous ones, and
shout for joy all you who are upright in heart."*

Psalm 32:11

*"Praise the Lord in **song**, for He has done excellent
things."*

Isaiah 12:5

*"And they shall **speak** of the glory of Thy kingdom, and
talk of Thy power."*

Psalm 145:11

Hands:

"*I will **bless** Thee as long as I live; I will **lift up my hands**
in Thy name.*"

Psalm 63:4

*"O **clap your hands**, all peoples; Shout to God with the
voice of joy."*

Psalm 47:1

Body:

*"Come let us **worship** and **bow down**; Let us **kneel** before*

the Lord our Maker. For He is our God."

Psalm 95:6

"And with a leap, he stood upright and began to walk; and he entered the temple with them, **walking** *and* **leaping** *and* **praising** *God."*

Acts 3:8

"Let them **praise** *His name with* **dancing***."*

Psalm 149:3

"Behold, **bless** *the Lord, all servants of the Lord, who* **serve** *by night in the house of the Lord."*

Psalm 134:1

Instruments:

"Praise Him with **trumpet** *sound; Praise Him with* **harp** *and* **lyre***. Praise Him with* **timbrel** *and dancing; Praise Him with* **stringed instruments** *and* **pipe***. Praise Him with* **loud cymbals***; Praise Him with* **resounding cymbals***."*

Psalm 150:3-5

When we praise and worship God through these avenues, it is, as we have mentioned, to be done with a heart full of thanksgiving and a sacrificial spirit - not to please men, but as a way of giving to God.

It behooves us now to start to experience the lifestyle of a true worshipper in today's world. We have thus far cited many Biblical examples of those who were intimate with God, but because of their remoteness, it is sometimes difficult to envision ourselves in their place. To show how these principles can be applied practically to every one of our lives, let us assume a privileged vantage point from which to view a day in the life of one such twentieth century worshipper. From there, what might we expect to see?

Early in the morning, long before the birds have even begun to greet the rising sun, our worshipper awakens. As he rubs the sleep from his eyes, he is heard saying, ''Thank you Lord, for one more day.'' During the next few moments as he throws off the covers, gets out of bed and takes care of personal needs, he hums softly a hymn of praise. Removing his Bible from its familiar spot on the nightstand, placed carefully there the previous evening before drifting off to sleep, he pads into the kitchen to reach for a glass of chilled fruit juice. Then, he's off to his favorite niche for spending precious moments with the Lord.

What had earlier begun as soft humming, now grows into joyful singing. Tenderly clasping his Bible close to his heart and walking back and forth, he is ever so thankful for all that God has done: the sacrifice and resurrection of Jesus, the cleansing power of the Blood, forgiveness, new life - freedom from the bondage of sin, and above all else, for eternal life with Him. Over the years, he has learned the blessings of openly expressing his feelings to the Lord. As his time of praise and gratitude continues, we see him clapping occasionally, lifting his hands, and upon a closer look, notice tears welling up in his eyes. Then something happens. God once again fulfills His promise to ''inhabit the praises of His people.''

In mid-stride, he comes to a standstill and stops singing. We can hear him whispering again and again, the name of Jesus, while in gentle reverence he lifts his hands, as if offering his very heart back to the Lord. The sweet communion he feels is evidenced by the tranquil glow on his face.

Slowly he kneels in front of the easy chair and lets his Bible fall open to the twenty-third Psalm. He reads the words in quiet affirmation of their truth. We hear him praying for his family, his pastor, church leaders around the world, and the nation's leaders, interceding on their behalf. His moving petitions flow forth, for their forgiveness and guidance, in each case according to the Scriptural promises laid up in his heart.

Last of all we hear him praying that he would be a better husband, a more faithful servant and a better steward of God's gifts, one able to see everything from God's perspective rather than his own. We can almost feel the fervor with which he pleads to be conformed to the image of Jesus. As he starts turning the well-worn and familiar pages of his Bible, we hear one last petition for himself, ''Lord, open my eyes, that I might behold wonders out of your law...quicken me according to your Word and feed me today my daily bread.''

Reaching into the drawer of the nearby end table, he brings forth his Bible study notebook and pen. He is prepared to receive God's directions for the day.

For the next hour or so he seems completely unaware of the passage of time. He reads, occasionally nodding his head and smiling, and then as a truth is revealed, exclaims, "Yes, Lord . . . .Hallelujah. . . .I praise You!" while he excitedly jots down lines in his notebook. Continuing in his daily Bible study, he moves to his desk, where, within easy reach are his favorite commentaries, a concordance and Bible dictionary. Surrounded by the ponderous volumes, he breathes a sigh of contentment. He realizes he still has half an hour to research the precious truths earlier revealed.

Time slips by, and much to his dismay, his favorite texts must be set aside until later. All too quickly the moment arrives to get ready for the challenges of a day's work. Leaving the room, he meets his wife, who has just come from her time of personal devotions, and greets her good morning with a warm kiss and embrace.

Arms still around each other, she says, "Oh, hon, I've got good news. I think the Lord has just given us an answer. Hurry up...get ready for work and we'll talk about it over breakfast." Humming softly to herself, she heads into the kitchen while he busies himself getting ready.

A short time later, his nose leading him to the source of the wonderful aroma wafting through the house, he wanders into the kitchen, Bible and notebook in one hand and jacket tossed casually over his shoulder. "Mmm...homemade muffins! That's just what I wanted this morning! Sweetheart, how'd you know?"

She smiles secretly, while setting a delicious breakfast before him and one at her own place. Taking her hand, they bow their heads and he invites the Lord to bless the food. "That was great, hon," he says finishing his meal. Sure am glad I married you!" Then he pauses. "Well, let's hear what the Lord showed you this morning during your prayer time. You seemed pretty excited a little while ago."

"I think we're supposed to go ahead. I feel right about it. The Lord seemed to be saying that now is the time for us to step out in faith."

Jumping up from her chair, she grabs his Bible, opens it and pointing to a verse, says, "I think this is our answer."

He chuckles aloud as his eyes slowly scan the words. Then he stands up and gives her a big hug. "Hon, let me show you what the Lord told me this morning," he grins as he picks up his notebook. He leads her over to their favorite loveseat, sits her down and puts his arm around her while opening the notebook on her lap. "Read this," he urges, indicating the passage.

She begins reading aloud, paying special attention to the words he had underlined, "Brethren, I count not myself to have apprehended; but this one thing I do, forgetting those things which are behind, and *reaching forth* unto those things which are before, I *press toward* the mark for the prize of the *high calling* of God in Christ Jesus. . ." She sets the notebook down and looks up at him with tears in her eyes. "That's...the exact verse... He gave me!"

In reply he declares, "The Lord sure is faithful, isn't he, hon?" "Well, it's settled. I'll call Pastor and tell him that we'll accept the offer to lead praise and worship. Let's pray now. It's almost time for me to go." They join hands and begin to pray for each other, calling upon God's protection and blessing. As they complete their special time together, they walk hand in hand to the front door for one last hug before he leaves for work.

Pulling into the space marked "maintenance supervisor" in the hospital parking lot, our worshipper pauses a moment to listen to the last strains of the praise music coming softly through the radio. Climbing out of the car, he grabs the card with his Scripture memory verse for the day and heads to his office. He is greeted enthusiastically by a co-worker awaiting their regular prayer group started years ago. "I really look forward to these few minutes we have before work," the other volunteers. "It sure makes a big difference."

Another worker wanders into the boiler room, and overhearing the conversation, adds, "Yeah, I don't know how we made it around here before you asked us to join you."

Morning passes quickly and lunch time arrives. He picks up his Bible and lunchbox packed carefully by his wife and heads for his favorite dining spot out by the pond. It's so peaceful there, watching the ducks at play in the water. He smiles when he finds the love note tucked underneath his sandwich, and breathes a prayer of thanks for such a wonderful companion. When he's done eating he reads some Psalms and Proverbs and concentrates on his memory verse until the end of the lunch hour.

The afternoon poses a few minor crises for him, most of which are handled with calm efficiency - a composure resulting from the assurance that Someone far greater than himself is in control. It wasn't always that way. Time was, when he rushed off to work late, in a dither of anxiety over what problems the day would bring. How well he knows that Jesus does, indeed, make a difference. His grace is always sufficient (II Corinthians 12:9).

Afternoon rush hour traffic on the way home, enough to make anybody backslide, is no longer the harrowing, white-knuckled experience it used to be. Instead, he offers the sacrifice of praise, singing familiar scripture songs of victory. He looks forward to the fellowship he and his wife will have that evening with some friends from church.

As he turns into their street, he hears the faint barking of a dog. At the driveway he is met by an exuberant bundle of four-legged energy. "Monarch! Are you glad to be back from the vet, old boy? I sure missed you this morning!"

Monarch continues to bark excitedly and run in circles, bounding and leaping about as he trots beside his master into the house. "I've got to call the Pastor right away and let him know of our decision," he says to himself. Once inside, he is greeted passionately by his sweetheart of 25 years who escorts him to his easy chair in the den.

"Supper will be ready soon, hon, so just relax here 'til then."

"Can you spare a moment to come sit with me while I make that call to Pastor? We're a team, so you need to be here." His thoughtfulness elicits a grateful smile from his wife and she perches on the arm of his chair. Monarch heaves a sigh of contentment as he rests nearby.

A short while after dinner, surrounded by their friends, they excitedly share how God spoke to them both that morning. They tell of how, for the past week, they had been seeking guidance concerning a major decision. True to His Word, they had asked and the Lord had given wisdom liberally. Knowing the responsibility involved in leading and teaching worship, they needed the assurance that it was, in fact, God's will for them.

Once the friends have all gone home and just the three of them

- husband, wife and faithful Monarch - are alone again, they relax on the loveseat as they share the events of the day and enjoy one another's presence. Opening their Bible one last time, they take turns reading aloud. Each offers insight into the passage and how it can be applied to their lives. Drawing to a close their time in the Word, they kneel down side by side, and, before retiring to bed, join together in prayer.

As we leave our vantage point, we find our worshipper and his wife giving thanks for the blessing of their deepening walk with the Lord, and looking forward in humble anticipation of the miracles yet to come.

What can we, who are learning to worship, discover from this story? It may serve as one example of our goal, which is to live life as a true worshipper. All of the major elements discussed thus far in the book come together in one practical illustration. This is not to say that we should strive to rigidly imitate this example. Worship varies from day to day and from person to person; there are no two days where it is exactly the same for any of us. However, in the story are scriptural dynamics that we can use as a guide in our own lives. Let us review these points:

God's invitation to worship extends to all. He is no respecter of persons. The main character was not someone extra-special, but an ordinary working man who loved the Lord and had learned to become a worshipper. Above all else, we find that God was the center around which his whole life revolved. In rising early in the morning, his very first thoughts were of the Lord. Like the psalmist David, there was an obvious hunger within him to commune with God, and he was more than willing to sacrifice a couple hours sleep. "O God, Thou art my God; *early* will I seek Thee: my soul *thirsteth* for Thee, my flesh *longeth* for Thee in a dry and thirsty land, where no water is" (Psalm 63:1). His inner heart attitude was one of humility and gratitude, freely expressed outwardly through his songs of praise that led him into worship and the presence of God. Although his relationship with the Lord was intimate, our worshipper still regarded Him with reverent awe.

This time of communion was followed by Spirit-inspired prayer for the needs of others, for himself to be more like Jesus, and for God's will to be accomplished in the earth. Waiting patiently upon the Lord, he prayed and read the Word expectantly, knowing God would provide guidance for his life. Next, he joyfully proceeded to a more in-depth study of the Bible in all its intricate beauty. To our worshipper, it was a source of unending fulfillment. The Word was so precious to him that he carried it to work, and even made out special cards with memory verses on them.

Love, born of worship, was eagerly shared with his cherished wife. She, too, followed his example in commitment to early morning devotions. They each knew they were a gift, one to another from the Father, who was their first love. Their lifestyle of worship gave birth to a desire to serve Him. As doors to ministry opened and God confirmed His will, they stepped forward in faith. Their waiting was not a hesitancy to serve, but an acknowledgment of their total dependence upon Him for their service to be fruitful. In fact, this interdependent relationship was evident throughout the day.

At work, his day began by asking God to be in control. This simple faith, so openly displayed as a light for those around him to see, resulted in calmness of spirit in spite of the circumstances that arose. Also, the joy of the Lord that filled his heart gave him a deeper appreciation for God's creation.

That evening was spent in fellowship with close Christian friends, encouraging one another in the Lord. Their day closed with prayer and the Word, this time, together, as a family. "*Evening*, and *morning*, and at *noon*, will I pray, and cry aloud: and He shall hear my voice" (Psalm 55:17). "I will bless the Lord at *all times*; His praise shall continually be in my mouth" (Psalm 34:1).

Yes, we are to unceasingly worship our wonderful Lord! When all is said and done, as Judson Cornwall stated, "Worship is best learned by worshipping."[33] What begins with the seed of decision in our heart and springs up to bud in the soil of everyday occurrences will come to full bloom as we find our place in congregational worship. Just as the bloom comes after the bud, so too, should our worship in the assembly be an outgrowth of our personal, daily worship. This thought is appropriately expressed by Allen and Borror,

> "...*all of life becomes a worship service. If Christians were devotedly practicing this lifestyle, a corporate*

service could not miss being a great blessing, for it would simply be a continuation of a worship service begun days (or weeks or months) before.''[34]

Chapter 9

Celebrating God Together

 s a thoughtful gift is a celebration of a birthday, as a special evening out is a celebration of an anniversary, as a warm eulogy is a celebration of life, as a sexual embrace is a celebration of a marriage - so a worship service is a celebration of God. ''[35]

We all treasure those times when the family gathers for such special occasions. Festivities shared with others we love lend a certain significance to life's major happenings, and serve to remind us that we're part of a group - a family. Behind every successful celebration lies much preparation, planning and effort. The same is true of the corporate celebration of God. This preparation is comparable to the effort which goes into developing a lifestyle of worship, culminating in the weekly worship service. ''We must understand that getting anything *out* of worship depends directly on our willingness to put effort *in* to it!''[36]

In our personal walk, this may mean allowing God to effect major changes in attitudes, habits, use of time, etc. That, in itself, is challenging enough, but when we come together in fellowship with other believers we face added difficulties. However great the challenge, it is well worth the effort. In the same way that a rose must be cultivated before its beautiful aroma can be enjoyed, the body of believers must undergo a similar process. Before the flower of worship will come to full bloom and emanate a heavenly fragrance, the ground must be prepared.

The world could not help but be drawn to, and affected by, the true Body of Christ that worships in harmony. Like the early church in the book of Acts who were in one accord, the Body of Christ today would then be better able to make an impact upon our world.

> *"And when they heard this, they lifted their voices to God*
> *with one accord and said, 'O Lord, it is Thou who didst*
> *make the heaven and the earth and the sea, and all that*
> *is in them...' And when they had prayed, the place where*
> *they had gathered together was shaken, and they were*
> *all filled with the Holy Spirit, and began to speak the*
> *word of God with boldness. And the congregation of those*
> *who believed were of one heart and one soul."*
>
> Acts 4:24,31,32a

"Many go to church. Few go to worship," was the heading on a church billboard in Nashville. How accurate that is! The Christian community worships in many ways, but is it the basis for all our activity? In the meetings there may be preaching, confession of sins and assurances of forgiveness, Scripture reading, communion and baptisms. The church sanctions marriages, participates in public prayer and sings hymns. We may even be known for our musical ability, but what lies at the core of all these experiences?

The worship of our Lord Jesus Christ must be at the center of every aspect of our lives. It is not enough that activities, functions and ceremonies take place in the name of Jesus if His presence does not permeate them. If the worship we experience does not give us "courage in the night, joy in the dawn" and power for service, then it is only a mere facsimile of the real thing. [37] Only when we do all in His name to glorify *Him*, are we approaching genuine worship.

> *"Worship is the one religious activity that lends itself to*
> *such a delicate blending of different heritages, for*
> *worship is so Christ-centered and requires such a God-*
> *consciousness that participants must look away from*
> *themselves in order to worship."* [38]

Unfortunately though, more strife occurs because of differences of opinion surrounding the concepts and performance of worship than perhaps any other area of our faith. As Christians, we all agree on certain basic doctrinal truths, but we must also constantly remind ourselves of the need for individuality in worship. As long as it lies within the bounds of Scripture, everyone should have the freedom to express their sincere, heartfelt love of God. We must remember that our way is not the only way. Others may be just as sincere and growing equally as close to the Lord.

Irregardless of our prior church experience, it is not easy to achieve a Scriptural balance in the dimensions that make up our love of God. We may remember from our study of the love triangles that *worship* is the motivational factor. It spurs us on to acquire increased *knowledge* and develop a stronger *covenant* with the Lord.

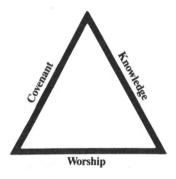

Worship

We noted the types of churches lacking in this all-important component of worship. Either a man-made ritualistic formula or a Pharisaical intellectualism characterizes the coldness of these assemblies. As we mentioned earlier, ritual is not all bad if it is used as a basis upon which worship is built. Congregational worship for the Old Testament Jews always began with ritual, proceeded on to worship and finally to oneness with God - one, two, three. Just as a man's bones give support and shape to his body, so too, can meaningful ritual draw people together and lend solidity to worship.

In contrast to the cold and dry churches, we found, on the opposite end of the scale, that an overabundance of worship without an equal measure of the two remaining elements is just as unhealthy in a body of believers. For us to develop a positive, growing love relationship with God, all three components must be of a harmonious emphasis! Indeed, maintaining this balance is difficult enough in our personal walk. What happens in a worshipping assembly?

During congregational worship, it is possible for our eyes to be focused on man rather than on God. If we find ourselves being distracted by the manner in which others worship, or if we allow our personal prejudice to hinder us, we will be unable to sense God's glory. Those of us who have been brought up in traditional denominations may tend to shy away from those with uplifted hands during prayer and worship. Yet, this should not be so, because the lifting up of our hands is only a symbol of releasing everything into God's more-than-capable hands. Besides, if the truth of the matter be known, there is much Scriptural support for this practice, while there is absolutely no Biblical precedent for the folding of hands.

"Lift up your hands in the sanctuary, and bless the Lord."
Psalm 134:2

"May my prayer be counted as incense before Thee; the lifting up my hands as the evening sacrifice."
Psalm 141:2

"Then Solomon stood before the altar of the Lord in the presence of all the assembly of Israel and spread out his hands toward heaven."
I Kings 8:22

"Therefore I want the men in every place to pray, lifting up holy hands, without wrath and dissension."
I Timothy 2:8

Setting aside preconceived notions and personal inhibitions is certainly not easy, but must be done. There may also be other things that occur during communal worship of which we may be rather intolerant. However, throughout the Scriptures there is a clear exhortation not to abandon the assembling of the brethren,

"Not forsaking our own assembling together, as is the habit of some, but encouraging one another; and all the more, as you see the day drawing near."
Hebrews 10:25

In every gathering of New Testament worshippers, we see, first of all, that they were committed followers of Jesus Christ. Christians today, as well as then, must come together in the name of Jesus, lest we should be likened to a man without a head. We have a thrilling promise to believe in and proclaim every time we gather in the precious name of the Lord of hosts,

> *"For where two or three have gathered together in My name, **there I am in the midst of them.**"*
>
> Matthew 18:20

When we look to the early church for enlightenment concerning these gatherings, we see some situations well worth noting. The first and most obvious is the fact that every assembly was self-governing, separated from the others because of distance only. In each locale, all believers came together as one group. Nowhere do we find reference to any such thing as denominations or religions, only believers and unbelievers. In fact, those who did attempt to separate for one reason or another were reprimanded by the apostle Paul,

> *"Now I exhort you, brethren, by the name of our Lord Jesus Christ, that you all agree, and there be no divisions among you, but you be made complete in the same mind and in the same judgment. Has Christ been divided? Paul was not crucified for you, was he? Or were you baptized in the name of Paul?"*
>
> I Corinthians 1:10,13

While adoration of God is still the primary purpose for congregational worship, mutual encouragement is another important reason for gathering together. Yet, this time of worship does not take place on a free-for-all basis. There should exist freedom of the Holy Spirit while maintaining certain principles of order, because God is not the author of confusion (I Corinthians 14:33).

Paul's epistle to the Ephesian church tells us to rejoice in the Spirit of God rather than seek earthly bliss,

> *"Speaking to one another in psalms and hymns and*

> *spiritual songs, singing and making melody with your*
> *heart to the Lord..."*
>
> Ephesians 5:19

The only restrictions that were placed upon the singing, dancing, shouting, weeping and spiritual gifts was for them to be done to the glory' of God and the edifying of His body. In the 14th chapter of I Corinthians we see guidelines concerning the use of spiritual gifts,

> *"What then is the outcome, brethren? When you assemble,*
> *each one has a psalm, has a teaching, has a revelation,*
> *has a tongue, has an interpretation. Let all things be done*
> *for edification. If anyone speaks in a tongue, it should*
> *be by two or at the most three, and each in turn, and*
> *let one interpret; but if there is no interpreter, let him*
> *keep silent in the church; and let him speak to himself*
> *and to God. And let two or three prophets speak, and*
> *the others pass judgment."*
>
> I Corinthians 14:26-29

In I Timothy, Paul encouraged reading the Scripture as an essential part of group worship,

> *"Until I come, give attention to the public reading of*
> *Scripture, to exhortation and teaching."*
>
> I Timothy 4:13

Paul also desired that his letters be read to the congregation and shared between the separate assemblies. This kept the lines of communication open and promoted evenly balanced growth throughout the entire body of Christ (I Thessalonians 5:27, Colossians 4:16).

Yes, it is true that all of these activities should be taking place during a worship service that is based upon Biblical principles. Unfortunately, most churches today are lacking in one or more of these areas. If we are to revitalize our love relationship with God, then we must seek to restore worship to its rightful position. Let us look to some Scriptural examples of congregational assemblies where the glory and power of God came to dwell.

The time was shortly after David, as king of Israel, defeated the Philistine army from Geba to Gazer, and brought the ark of God to the city of Jerusalem. The whole nation of Israel turned out for this great event. The entire account is described in II Samuel 6, but we will concentrate on those verses pertaining to worship,

> *"Now David again gathered all the chosen men of Israel, thirty thousand. Meanwhile, David and all the house of Israel were celebrating before the Lord with all kinds of instruments made of fir wood, and with lyres, harps, tambourines, castanets and cymbals. And so it was, that when the bearers of the ark of the Lord had gone six paces, he sacrificed an ox and a fatling. And David was dancing before the Lord with all his might, and David was wearing a linen ephod. So David and all the house of Israel were bringing up the ark of the Lord with shouting and the sound of the trumpet. So they brought in the ark of the Lord and set it in its place inside the tent which David had pitched for it; and David offered burnt offerings and peace offerings before the Lord. And when David had finished offering the burnt offering and the peace offering, he blessed the people in the name of the Lord of hosts."*
>
> II Samuel 6:5,13-15,17,18

Although freedom and joy was evident in their worship there was order in everything that took place, despite the criticism of King David's wife for his lack of formality.

Another example of superb congregational worship occurred when Solomon dedicated the newly-completed temple. The ark of the covenant had been set in its position of reverence in the holy of holies and the following took place,

> *"And when the priests came forth from the holy place (for all the priests who were present had sanctified themselves, without regard to divisions), and all the Levitical singers, Asaph, Herman, Jeduthun and their*

sons and kinsmen, clothed in fine linen, with cymbals,
harps, and lyres, standing east of the altar, and with them
one hundred twenty priests blowing trumpets in unison
when the trumpeters and the singers were to make
themselves heard with one voice accompanied by
trumpets and cymbals and instruments of music, and
when they praised the Lord saying, 'He indeed is good
for His lovingkindness is everlasting,' then the house,
the house of the Lord, was filled with a cloud, so that
the priests could not stand to minister because of the
cloud, **for the glory of the Lord filled the house of God."**
II Chronicles 5:11-14

At this point Solomon addressed all of the people and blessed
them as they stood before the Lord. After a brief word to them,
Solomon prayed,

"...kneeled down upon his knees before all the
congregation of Israel, and spread forth his hands toward
heaven."
II Chronicles 6:13b

After they fulfilled God's requirements for coming into His
presence, we see God's, as well as the peoples' response,

"Now when Solomon had finished praying, fire came down
from heaven and consumed the burnt offering and the
sacrifices and the glory of the Lord filled the house. And
the priests could not enter into the house of the Lord,
because the glory of the Lord filled the Lord's house.
And all the sons of Israel, seeing the fire come down and
the glory of the Lord upon the house, bowed down on
the pavement with their faces to the ground, and they
worshipped and gave praise to the Lord, saying, 'Truly
He is good, truly His lovingkindness is everlasting.' "
II Chronicles 7:1-3

When the presence of Almighty God descended, it was so

awesome that the priests could not even enter the temple. Imagine how great must have been the glory, how humbling to all those present! They knew that there was a God whose name was Jehovah. Their only response was worship.

Let us look at one more model of true, communal worship. The setting was the time of the rebuilding of Jerusalem recounted in the book of Nehemiah,

> *"And all the people gathered as one man at the square which was in front of the Water Gate, and they asked Ezra the scribe to bring the book of the law of Moses which the Lord had given to Israel. Then Ezra the priest brought the law before the assembly of men, women, and all who could listen with understanding...and he read from it before the square which was in front of the Water Gate from early morning until midday...and all the people were attentive to the book of the law. And Ezra blessed the Lord, the great God. And all the people answered, 'Amen, Amen!' while lifting up their hands; then they bowed low and worshipped the Lord with their faces to the ground. Also Jeshua...and the Levites explained the law to the people while the people remained in their place. And they read from the book, from the law of God, translating to give the sense so that they understood the reading. Then Nehemiah, who was the governor, and Ezra the priest and scribe, and the Levites who taught the people said to all the people, 'This day is holy to the Lord your God; do not mourn or weep.' For all the people were weeping when they heard the words of the law.''*
>
> Nehemiah 8:1,3,5-9

We find here, then, as in the words of John MacArthur,

> *"Worship is not an emotional exercise with God-words that induce certain feelings. Worship is a response built upon truth...If we are to worship in truth, and the Word of God is truth, we must worship out of an understanding*

of the Word of God.''[39]

In this passage, we can see the tremendous power of the Scriptures when read and explained to an assembly under the anointing of the Holy Spirit. It moved them so much that they wept. Oh, that we would have such power behind our teaching today!

The importance of saints gathered together in worship cannot be mistaken. When all the examples we have looked at are taken as a whole, a pattern for congregational worship evolves. What, though, does this have to do with us, we might wonder? Since these illustrations were in the Old Testament, do they apply to us today?

It is quite true that we now live under a new covenant with the Father. No longer are we bound by the regimen of the law, but enjoy grace by faith in Jesus. As we have stated, the manner in which God deals with us now is different than it was with the children of Israel prior to the birth, death and resurrection of the Lord Jesus. Yet, neither His principles nor His desires have changed,

> *"For I, the Lord, do not change; therefore you, O sons of Jacob, are not consumed."*
>
> Malachi 3:6

> *"Jesus Christ is the same yesterday and today, yes and forever."*
>
> Hebrews 13:8

In his book **Real Worship**, Warren Wiersbe was asked basically this same question and his reply, in part, was as follows,

> *"The Old Testament legal ceremonies were fulfilled in Christ, so we do not repeat them today. But I see no reason why we must make an artificial distinction between "Old Testament worship" and "New Testament worship" when we see no such distinction in Scripture.''*[40]

From the aforementioned patterns of worship, some all-important truths can be derived. The most outstanding feature concerning worship is that, in each case, it took place in response to a manifestation or revelation of the glory of the Lord. It burst forth from the hearts of the people in a manner comparable to that of a river overcoming a dam. How much more true should this be for us today, who have the Spirit of God dwelling in our hearts? A.P. Gibbs rendered the following beautiful description of the source and destination of this spiritual river within us,

"Christ used the analogy of living water to describe the spiritual life which He came to make possible to all who believe,

'Everyone who drinks of this water shall thirst again; but whoever drinks of the water that I shall give him shall become in him a well of water springing up to eternal life.'

John 4:13,14

This living water comes in to the believer at the new birth. It springs up, within him, in worship. It then flows out, from him, in service.

'If any man is thirsty, let him come to Me and drink. He who believes in Me, as the Scripture said, From his innermost being shall flow rivers of living water.'

John 7:37-39

Thus worship really consists of this living water returning to its source. Long ago Solomon made the discovery that though all the rivers ran into the sea, yet the sea did not become any fuller thereby. He correctly assigned the reason as follows:

'All the rivers flow into the sea, yet the sea is not full. To the place where the rivers flow, there they flow again.'

Ecclesiastes 1:7,8"

For this river to flow unhindered through us it must first be returned, in worship, to its ultimate Source. "Thus, the spiritual life which flows from God to us returns to Him in worship from us, and thus the divine cycle is complete."[41]

Chapter 10

Obstacles and Pitfalls

*T*here are giants in the land of worship. "God names the giants...presents His battle strategy and leads on to victory. Worship is worth the warfare."[42] Such dangers have as their source, as quoted by A.P. Gibbs, one or more of the following three things, "the devil, the infernal enemy, the world, the external enemy, and the flesh, the internal enemy."[43]

In II Corinthians, Paul classified all mankind into three groups: the natural, the carnal and the spiritual man. The reknowned 20th century Chinese preacher and teacher of the Word, Watchman Nee, wrote extensively on this subject. In his three-volume series, *The Spiritual Man*, he defined these groups. Natural man is separated from God as a result of Adam's sin and ensuing fall from grace. Carnal or soulish man is redeemed from eternal death by belief in the blood of Jesus Christ. He has the Holy Spirit living within him, but his life is ruled by the flesh, mind, will or emotions. The spiritual man is totally submitted to the Holy Spirit. His human spirit, led by the Spirit of God, directs his body and soul (mind, will and emotions).

Natural man cannot worship because he has no relationship with God; He is Creator, but not Lord. Carnal or soulish man cannot experience true worship because he is swayed too often by intellectualism, emotionalism and his own human desires. It is spiritual man alone who worships in the beauty of holiness, because his spirit, communing directly with the Spirit of God, is completely yielded to His leading.

God has placed within every born-again believer the desire to worship, but the carnal man, because he does not walk in the Spirit, is continually ensnared by the obstacles

111

and pitfalls to worship. As Christians, we must be in the world, but not of it, saying "no" to the selfish things of life and "yes" to God and His commandments. To become true worshippers, we need to maintain that all-important balance in our love relationship with God, and be willing to leave behind every obstacle and pitfall as vanquished foes. There is no other way.

Pride

Pride completely excludes worship and is our greatest single stumbling-block.

> "*Pride is a subtle thing and often exists where it is least expected, for one can even be proud of his humility! Pride in one's own personal appearance leads that individual to give undue attention to himself, or herself. Pride of gift leads to an ostentatious display of it and a secret craving for applause. Pride of position leads its owner to adopt a condescending air to his fellow believers. Pride of possessions shows itself in self-complacency and boasting. Pride of one's ecclesiastical position evidences itself in smugness and sanctimoniousness.*"[44]

It was this very same fault that led to Lucifer's rebellion against God,

> "*How you have fallen from heaven, O star of the morning, son of the dawn! You have been cut down to the earth, you who have weakened the nations! But you said in your heart, 'I will ascend to heaven; I will raise my throne above the stars of God, and I will sit on the mount of assembly in the recesses of the north. I will ascend above the heights of the clouds; I will make myself like the Most High.'*"

Isaiah 14:12-15

Lucifer was the very leader of worship in heaven, walking closest to the throne of the Almighty, until he became prideful and wanted to take His place,

*"You were the anointed cherub who covers (the throne),
and I placed you there. You were on the holy mountain
of God; You walked in the midst of the stones of fire.
You were blameless in your ways from the day you were
created, until unrighteousness was found in you."*
Ezekiel 28:14,15

Closely associated with pride is self-will. We see an example
of this obstacle in reference to two of Aaron, the high priest's, sons.
These men knew the commandments of God regarding proper
worship, yet they willfully disobeyed and paid a heavy price,

*"Now Nadab and Abihu, the sons of Aaron, took their
respective firepans, and after putting fire in them, placed
incense on it and offered strange fire before the Lord,
which He had not commanded them. And fire came out
from the presence of the Lord and consumed them, and
they died before the Lord."*
Leviticus 10:1,2

Rebellious pride is costly, and at the very least, destroys true
worship which is pleasing to God. We must come to Him on His
terms, not ours.

Lack of Knowledge

We may remember from our study of the love triangles that a
lack of Scriptural knowledge may not only keep us from true worship;
it may allow us to be led astray, sometimes with harmful results.
In Hosea, we see that a lack of knowledge was no excuse for
disobedience. As the Scripture says, "My people are destroyed for
lack of knowledge" (Hosea 4:6). King David's disastrous first
attempt to restore the ark of God to Jerusalem is a prime example.
If we remember, the ark represented the presence of God, where
He communed with his people through the high priest during
worship.

It was plainly written in the Scriptures that only Aaron and his sons could touch the holy things of the tabernacle, while the sons of Kohath were to carry the ark only on poles placed through rings on the top,

> *"And when Aaron and his sons have finished covering the holy objects and all the furnishings of the sanctuary, when the camp is to set out, after that the sons of Kohath shall come to carry them, so they may not touch the holy objects and die. These are the things in the tent of meeting which the sons of Kohath are to carry."*
>
> Numbers 4:15

Since the ark had been missing from the house of Israel for many years, the divinely prescribed method for transporting it had been forgotten. What actually took place with King David's first attempt to restore the ark to the children of Israel is recorded in I Samuel,

> *"And they placed the ark of God on a new cart so that they might bring it . . . But when they came to the threshing floor of Nacon, Uzzah reached out toward the ark of God and took hold of it, for the oxen nearly upset it. And the anger of the Lord burned against Uzzah, and God struck him down there for his irreverence, and he died there by the ark of God."*
>
> II Samuel 6:6,7

It was of little importance that they tried to use a new cart to take the ark to Jerusalem, or that they had good intentions in wanting to restore it there in the first place. Although God does look at our heart in preparation for worship, obedience to His previously stated commands is also important. We should be so thankful for the blood of Jesus, which cleanses us so that our sins might not keep us from the presence of a Holy God.

Independence

We have already used the expression "interdependence" and made note that it is developed as our relationship with God deepens.

An independent spirit will not long be tolerated in the presence of God. Wanting to be self-reliant and able to succeed on our own skills is nothing less than sin. As teenagers, we all desired to be "grown-up" and out on our own in the world, independent from both God and family. It is during this period in life that many young Christians will stray from the Father's embrace and attempt to "do their own thing." It is also during this time that many great, and sometimes tragic, mistakes are made as a result of a search for independence.

This is the exact opposite of abiding (making our dwelling) in God and His abiding in us. That is why Jesus said that unless we become like little children, totally submissive and dependent, we cannot enter His kingdom. Perhaps God's reason for telling us to raise our hands in worship is as an outward indication of our inner dependency on Him, much like little ones who ask to be picked up and held by a parent.

Critical Spirit

The habit of finding fault with everything and everyone is devastating to worship. It is contrary to the attitudes and actions of Jesus who seeks to deliver us from our sinful ways rather than condemn us. When we criticize a brother, we are in essence condemning not only him, but ourselves as well,

> *"Therefore you are without excuse, every man of you who passes judgment, for in that you judge another, you condemn yourself."*
>
> Romans 2:1

Many times the faults that we see in others are those that trouble us. A critical spirit will certainly prevent us from becoming worshippers because it continually draws our gaze off of the perfection of God and onto the imperfections of mere men, especially *other* men. As long as we're pointing out another's weaknesses, we are not allowing God to cleanse us from our own sin, which, as we have seen, is a prerequisite to entering His presence.

*"Then you will call, and the Lord will answer; You will cry, and He will say, 'Here I am.' If you remove the yoke from your midst, the **pointing of the finger**..."*

Isaiah 58:9

Laziness

Worship is active, not passive. Laziness should not even be in the vocabulary of a true worshipper. Instead, there should be found in it such words as seek, search, guard, fight, run, plant, sow, reap, build and work...work...more work.

"But prove yourselves to be doers of the word, and not merely hearers who delude themselves."

James 1:22

Poor is he who works with a negligent hand, but the hand of the diligent makes rich."

Proverbs 10:4

In Matthew 25 is the story of a man taking a trip. Before leaving, he entrusted to three servants varying sums of money: five talents, two and one respectively. Two of the servants used what they were given wisely and multiplied it, while the third simply buried his.

Upon the man's return, the two who were fruitful were rewarded plentifully, while the third was cast from his master's presence,

"But his master answered and said to him, 'You wicked, lazy slave, you knew that I reap where I did not sow, and gather where I scattered no seed. ...Therefore take away the talent from him, and give it to the one who has the ten talents. For to everyone who has shall more be given, and he shall have in abundance, but from the one who does not have, even what he does have shall be taken away. And cast out the worthless slave into the outer darkness; in that place there shall be weeping and gnashing of teeth.' "

Matthew 25:26,28-30

These examples, although given in terms of material wealth, speak also of spiritual treasure. We, as "joint heirs with Jesus," have been given much to be used for the glory of God. In order for the spiritual treasure we have received to be multiplied, and for us to be deemed good and faithful servants, we must work with what we have been given. Like the two faithful servants who were diligent in their stewardship, looking expectantly for their master's return, we cannot simply passively await the return of our Master and expect to be blessed. The spiritually lazy person is not prepared to enter the presence of God. A worshipful life requires much effort and self-sacrifice. Spiritual slothfulness can result if we consider worship a duty to be performed, rather than a passionate response to a loving God. When this occurs, either individually or collectively, the fires of love begin to dim and grow cold.

Impatience

Failure to wait on God's go-ahead and presumptuously taking things into our own hands greatly hinders our relationship with Him. We are directed to "rest in the Lord and wait patiently for Him" (Psalm 37:7) and to "be still and know that He is God" (Psalm 46:10). We must learn to say with the Psalmist,

> *"My soul, wait in silence for God only, for my hope is from Him."*
>
> Psalm 62:5

Impatience, in direct opposition to God's commands, may lead to even greater sins. Saul, the king of Israel, was guilty of such a weakness while awaiting the return of Samuel, the prophet. It was Samuel's duty as a priest to lead the sacrificial worship before the armies engaged in battle, but Saul, in his impatience, overstepped his bounds and decided to perform the ceremony himself. This one act had far-reaching consequences,

> *"Now he waited seven days, according to the appointed time set by Samuel, but Samuel did not come to Gilgal; and the people were scattering from him. So Saul said,*

*'Bring to me the burnt offering and the peace offerings'
and he offered the burnt offering. And it came about as
soon as he finished offering the burnt offering, that
behold, Samuel came; and Saul went out to meet him
and to greet him. And Samuel said to Saul, 'You have
acted foolishly; you have not kept the commandment of
the Lord you God, which He commanded you, for now
the Lord would have established your kingdom over Israel
forever. But now your kingdom shall not endure. The
Lord has sought out for Himself a man after His own
heart...''*

I Samuel 13:8,9,13

As disastrous as was Saul's failure to wait upon God, so it is
for us. Worship cannot be rushed. We should never be in too much
of a hurry to practice the presence of God.

Performance Orientation

Do we find ourselves doing more and worshipping less? Are we
unable to find time to sing and praise the Lord or to rest quietly
in His presence? The need to constantly be doing something may
be associated with the sin of pride. We might be seeking fulfillment
through our works instead of the finished work of Christ. Being a
responsible ''Martha'' is important, but not to the extent that it
interferes with our ability to listen, worship and grow in the love
of God. Let us look at the words of Jesus to Mary and Martha,

*''And she had a sister called Mary, who moreover was
listening to the Lord's word, seated at His feet. But
Martha was distracted with all her preparations; and she
came up to Him, and said, 'Lord, do You not care that
my sister has left me to do all the serving alone? Then
tell her to help me.' But the Lord answered and said to
her, 'Martha, Martha, you are worried and bothered
about so many things; but only a few things are
necessary, really **only** one, for Mary has chosen the good
part, which shall not be taken away from her.' ''*

Luke 10:39-42

Emotionalism

Our human emotions may hinder the development of a worshipper's heart if they are allowed to rule unchecked by wisdom. Different emotions may affect people in various ways. Unfortunately, the majority have either long or short-range negative aspects. Anxiety and depression are two with which most of us have, at one time or another, had at least a passing acquaintance.

During the rebuilding of the temple at Jerusalem, the people reacted emotionally to the enemy's efforts to hinder their project. They became discouraged and unable to work,

> *"Thus in Judah it was said, 'The strength of the burden bearers is failing, yet there is much rubbish; and we ourselves are unable to rebuild the wall.''*
>
> Nehemiah 4:10

Professionalism

The evil of professionalism in the church is a distinct departure from the truth of God's Word and has wrought havoc among the body of Christ. Where the priesthood of believers has been exchanged for the exclusivity of the clergy, it has very nearly destroyed the church's ability to worship. Bradbent's *Pilgrim Church*, points out how, by forming a special ''caste'' among Christians called ''clergy,'' some mainline denominations have departed from the spirit of the New Testament church. Through His victory on the cross, Jesus established the ''priesthood of all believers.'' This was made clear when the veil between the holy and the most holy place was torn in two at the moment of His death,

> *"You also, as living stones, are being built up as a spiritual house for a holy priesthood to offer up spiritual sacrifices acceptable to God through Jesus Christ...but you are a chosen race, a royal priesthood, a holy nation, a people for God's own possession, that you may proclaim the excellencies of Him who has called you out of darkness into His marvelous light.''*
>
> I Peter 2:9

Tradition

Many times worship is compromised by theology instead of theology being permeated with worship. Endless questions about methods and other non-essentials detract from worship, stifling both our faith and love of God. Formalism, the outward observance of forms, rules and regulations may, when carried to extremes, quench the Spirit of God. We must be careful that our traditions enhance, rather than hinder, our worship.

Judson Cornwall summed up this idea when he said,

> *"To insist upon doing only what comes naturally is to limit ourselves to the peer pressure and cultural restraints others have placed upon us, and this means that we will never rise to a level higher than that which others have chosen for us to attain. Christ Jesus came to release us from every bondage and limitation that has kept us from Him, but it will take some conscious cooperation from us to enter into that freedom."*[45]

> *"Now the Lord is the Spirit; and where the Spirit of the Lord is, there is liberty."*
>
> II Corinthians 3:17

Worldly Influence

The flower of worship will never bloom in the soil of worldliness. The reason for this is simple; no man can serve two masters. Once we have been born again by the Spirit of the Lord we are no longer of this world and must not yield to its seeming attractions. Yet, its influence can creep into our lives insidiously if we are unaware of its dangers. For this reason Jesus prayed,

> *"I do not ask Thee to take them out of the world, but to keep them from the evil one. They are not of the world, even as I am not of the world."*
>
> John 17:15,16

"Do not love the world, nor the things in the world. If anyone loves the world, the love of the Father is not in him. For all that is in the world, the lust of the flesh and the lust of the eyes and the boastful pride of life, is not from the Father, but is from the world."

I John 2:15,16

Because of the strong pull of the world, we are advised to not even fellowship, much less join with, those involved in its pursuits. Although we are called to minister to them that they might receive Christ, we must remain free from their entanglements. Concerning this costly influence, we see one more admonition from the apostle Paul,

"Do not be bound together with unbelievers; for what partnership have righteousness and lawlessness, or what fellowship has light with darkness? Therefore, come out from their midst and be separate, says the Lord..."

II Corinthians 6:17

This separation is more than just an outward physical separation from the things of the world, but also includes the realm of our thought life. We can sit in church and, from all outward appearances, be gloriously worshipping the Lord while our mind is busy with the cares of the world. We cannot be mentally planning a business trip or thinking about the latest sale at the mall and still truly worship. God demands our all!

We should consider Lot's wife and the influence the evil city of Sodom held over her. When the family was commanded to leave Sodom before the Lord would destroy it by fire, she looked back and was destroyed along with the rest of the city. Though attractively camouflaged, the things of the world are used by Satan for one ultimate goal - to cause us to spend eternity in the lake of fire. Thus, if we choose to fellowship with darkness we will never be able to have sweet communion in worship with God, who is Light.

Humanism

In 1933, the first Humanist Manifesto suggested that the universe was self-existent and not created. It declared that there should be no unique religious emotions and attitudes of the kind associated with a belief in the supernatural. The humanists denied the spiritual foundation upon which our nation was built. They considered the religious forms and ideas of our forefathers inappropriate, and said that man alone was responsible for the realization of his dreams. Contained within man, himself, was the power for achievement. They were bold enough to suggest that God was dead and man supreme. How contrary to the Scriptures which say, "It is better to trust in the Lord than to put confidence in man" (Psalm 118:8).

Humanistic philosophy is running rampant throughout society today. Everywhere we turn there are people in love with themselves who, rejoicing in their abilities and accomplishments, give no glory whatsoever to God. Instead, we hear of self-improvement courses, self-esteem, self-will, self, self, self! What could hinder worship more than an attitude of man's sovereignty? If we are ever to be worshippers of the living God, every root of this demonic philosophy must be eradicated from our lives.

Unforgiveness

Harboring unforgiveness against anyone, whether for real or imagined wrongs, will hinder worship. In order to enter God's presence, we must be forgiven and cleansed from all sin,

> *"Behold, the Lord's hand is not so short that it cannot save; neither is His ear so dull that it cannot hear. But your iniquities have made a separation between you and your God, and your sins have hidden His face from you, so that He does not hear."*
>
> Isaiah 59:1,2

We cannot be forgiven if we will not forgive others their offenses. This truth is spoken by our Lord in the Sermon on the Mount,

> *"And forgive us our debts, as we also have forgiven our debtors...for if you forgive men for their transgressions, your heavenly Father will also forgive you. But if you*

do not forgive men, then your heavenly Father will not forgive your transgressions."

Matthew 6:12,13

Unforgiveness is devastating to our relationship with God. Whether in the Old Testament or in the New, the Word states that the only way to come into the presence of God is with the heart cleansed first from all sin. Until we choose to forgive everyone of everything, we will be unable to worship.

Pitfalls

Pitfalls are those dangerous habits or beliefs that may ensnare us as we continue on the path to worship. When anything assumes a higher priority in our lives than God, it is as if we have fallen into a pit and lost sight of our first love. If this occurs, we are guilty of idolatry. Many think, falsely, that idolatry is simply the pagan practice of bowing to statues, but it is much more common than that. The foremost commandments of the Lord are,

"Hear, O Israel! The Lord is our God, the Lord is one! And you shall love the Lord your God with all your heart and with all your soul and with all your might."

Deuteronomy 6:4,5

"Thou shalt have no other gods before me."

Exodus 20:3

Anything that causes us to break these commands is an inappropriate object of worship, in other words, an idol. It is essential that our priorities be brought back into the proper perspective. To protect ourselves against idolatry it is important that we know who is behind the scenes attempting to steal what rightfully belongs only to God. Satan would try to replace God as the lord of our heart and have us bow in obeisance to him. The devil even tempted Jesus at the beginning of His earthly ministry,

"Again, the devil took Him to a very high mountain, and

showed Him all the kingdoms of the world, and their glory; and he said to Him, 'All these things will I give You, if You fall down and worship me.' "

Matthew 4:8,9

We have already observed, from reading of Lucifer's fall from heaven, that pride was the cause of his downfall. In this conversation with Jesus, he was up to his old tactics in attempting to get the Lord to worship him. He will try the same thing with us today.

Most of us, when we think of idols, think of something of substance that can be touched with our hands, such as the false gods of pagan religions. These are idols, yet more often than not, modern idolatry takes on a far subtler form in our heart rather than our hands. Satan's attempts to steal our worship of the one true God are extremely deceptive and rarely take the form of a direct frontal attack. Instead, he prefers to sneak in the side door, catching us unaware. Therefore, to help expose his strategy, we will look briefly at some of these areas where we are most vulnerable.

Self

Far too often we find that we are our own worst enemy. Our society, especially in America, promotes a philosophy of immediate self-gratification as one of the highest standards of living. One can even find a magazine titled, ''Self'' on nearly every magazine rack today. We cannot be humble enough before God to worship Him if we are ruled by our own personal desires, especially if they conflict with the commands of God. Let us notice again the tactics Satan will use. In his temptation of Eve, Satan attacked her in the area of her self-centered desires,

"When the woman saw that the tree was good for food, and that it was a delight to the eyes, and that the tree was desirable to make one wise, she took from its fruit and ate; and she gave also to her husband with her, and he ate."

Genesis 3:6

Unless we are to succumb to the same subtle temptations, we must deny ourselves, take up our cross and follow the Lord Jesus with all our heart. This may be the most difficult thing for us to do, but let us consider the extent to which Jesus denied Himself for us. With every fiber of His being crying for life, He submitted to His Father's will and died, that we might live.

Family

In the Bible, there is much said about the family relationship. It is actually symbolic of Jesus and the Church. Husbands are to love their wives as Christ loved the Church and wives are to submit to and respect their husbands as the Church reverences Christ. We, in turn, are to train up our children according to scriptural principles of authority, bringing them up in the "discipline and instruction of the Lord." Anytime God's divine order is not followed, the result is confusion. An idol has been formed when our children's desires become more important than God's commands. In the story of Eli, a priest of Israel, he was prevented from worshipping the Lord as was his duty because he had allowed his sons to control him. The Lord told the prophet Samuel in a vision,

> *"In that day I will carry out against Eli all that I have spoken concerning his house, from beginning to end. For I have told him that I am about to judge his house forever for the iniquity which he knew, because his sons brought a curse on themselves and he did not rebuke them. And therefore I have sworn to the house of Eli that the iniquity of Eli's house shall not be atoned for by sacrifice or offering forever."*

I Samuel 3:12-14

Possessions

The things that we own - our home, cars, clothes, or items of convenience - may become idols. The key to preventing this is to realize that we are only stewards of any possessions and not the true owners; it is our Father in heaven to whom all things truly belong.

In Matthew 6:19-21, Jesus taught the value of maintaining the proper priority regarding possessions,

> *"Do not lay up for yourselves treasures upon earth, where moth and rust destroy, and where thieves break in and steal. But lay up for yourselves treasures in heaven, where neither moth nor rust destroys, and where thieves do not break in or steal; for where your treasure is, there will your heart be also."*

Believers in the book of Acts realized this fact and conducted their lives accordingly, sharing everything they had with one another,

> *"And the congregation of those who believed were of one heart and soul; and not one of them claimed that anything belonging to him was his own; but all things were common property to them...for there was not a needy person among them, for all who were owners of land or houses would sell them and bring the proceeds of the sales."*

Acts 4:32,34

During those days, the greatest revival of worship in history took place. Signs and wonders were prevalent and everyone spoke the Word of God with boldness. It must have been a glorious time when the Holy Spirit moved so powerfully among men!

Power

"Power corrupts, and absolute power corrupts absolutely," was well-stated by a wise man. This expression is just as true for today's church as it is for those involved in the world's system. As believers, we are all just parts of the body of Christ and He alone is the all-powerful Head. Even in the early church there were those who hungered for control over others, as we read of Diotrephes, who sought the prominent position,

> *"I wrote something to the church; but Diotrephes, who*

*loves to be first among them, does not accept what we
say."*

3 John 9

Compare this to Jesus' answer to a mother's request for her sons'
promotion,

> *"You know that the rulers of the Gentiles lord it over them,
> and their great men exercise authority over them. It is
> not so among you, but whoever wishes to become great
> among you shall be your servant, and whoever wishes
> to be first among you shall be your slave; just as the Son
> of Man did not come to be served, but to serve, and to
> give His life a ransom for many."*

Matthew 20:25-28

Let us continually examine and re-examine our motives to insure
that our desire is service, rather than a position of power. God alone
is boss and we, like Paul, must be His love slaves if we want to
be worshippers after His own heart.

Money

Money is the scoreboard most often worshipped in today's
society. How many of us have been quietly looking to Wall Street
and studying the stock market, rather than looking toward Jesus and
studying His Word? It is not money that causes problems, but the
love of it (I Timothy 6:10). When we allow the hunger for money
to become an idol in our lives, it keeps us from a relationship with
the Lord. Let us consider the tragic story of Ananias and Sapphira
in the book of Acts. It was during the time when the power of the
Holy Spirit was so mighty that people were led to sell their land
and possessions in order to give the money to the Lord's work. There
was no one among them who lacked anything because of their
obedience. Ananias and Sapphira were obedient in selling their land,
but they stumbled when the time came to part with the money,

> *"But Peter said, 'Ananias, why has Satan filled your heart*

> *to lie to the Holy Spirit, and to keep back some of the*
> *price of the land?...Why is it that you have conceived*
> *this deed in your heart? You have not lied to men, but*
> *to God.' And as he heard these words, Ananias fell down*
> *and breathed his last..."*
>
> Acts 5:3,4b,5

Sapphira's love of money caused her to follow in the steps of her husband and she also suffered the same fatal consequences. If we allow money to become an idol, it will lead us farther and farther from God and destroy any possibility of true worship. Let us heed these words, then, and steer clear of the danger associated with the love of money. May our treasure be devoted to the God we worship and to the spreading of the gospel of Jesus Christ.

Occupation

Before we come to experience the joy of true worship, some of us find the business world much more exciting. America is notorious for encouraging us to place success in our work above all else. People often feel condemned if they aren't at their jobs twelve hours a day. "God's Word recognizes the necessity for the Christian to be in business, but warns against business being in the Christian."[46] The apostle Paul, a tentmaker by trade (Acts 18:3), used his job as a means of helping to support his ministry. Paul did not order his ministry around his job and neither should we. Whether in full-time Christian service or not, we are to be good stewards who will use our occupations to enhance *God's* business - the preaching of the gospel to the world.

Recreation

God has planned that we should enjoy the fruit of our labor. When the enjoyment of this fruit becomes the sole purpose for laboring, idolatry, like a weed, has taken root. He is not a stern taskmaster who requires constant work; however, in our society, recreation may be the biggest competitor for quality time with Him. When sports and recreation, in themselves inherently beneficial, prevent us from reading the Bible, or from praying and worshipping God, they have become idols.

How much time and money is spent in search of that elusive quality, pleasure? Recreation offered by the world today is remotely removed from the Scriptural and is of no little concern to me. I am apprehensive about the effects of this on my children and future grandchildren because I know that even the best counterfeit is but a poor substitute for time with the Lord. Our recreation should glorify God and allow us to worship Him in a more Biblically sound way.

Paul, who in his illustrations of the Christian life, made references to a runner in a race as well as a skilled boxer, gave us the key to balance,

> *"For bodily discipline is only of little profit, but godliness*
> *is profitable for all things, since it holds promise for the*
> *present life and also for the life to come."*

I Timothy 4:8

Recreation and good physical health should enhance our ability to worship, but by no means should ever replace it.

Science

In today's world of increasing technology, science has become an idol - the one used most often to refute the truth of the Bible. When the wisdom of this world is divorced from the knowledge of God, it may oppose the divine revelation found in the Scriptures. If we choose to place our faith in science above the truth of God's Word, we are guilty of idolatry.

Many of us are familiar with the conflict currently taking place in our nation's schools concerning the theory of evolution as opposed to Biblical creationism. Much of this debate rages around the seeming discrepancy between the age of the earth and the length of man's existence on the planet. Yet, a closer look reveals the total awesomeness of our God and declares the absolute truthfulness of His Word. Let us pursue this point a bit further in support of our glorious Lord.

As we first open our Bibles, we see in Genesis 1:1 that, "In the

beginning God created the heavens and the earth.'' Here, then, is
the ultimate beginning of creation; prior to this in the dateless past,
God alone existed. When He created heaven and earth, included were
all the stars, the sun and moon, the earth and all the heavenly host:
angels, cherubim, seraphim and even that anointed cherub himself,
Lucifer.

In the fourteenth chapter of Isaiah and in the twenty-eighth chapter
of Ezekiel, we read more about the fall of Lucifer and learn that
he was cast from heaven into the earth,

> *"How art thou fallen from heaven, O Lucifer, son of the*
> *morning! how art thou cut down to the ground..."*
>
> Isaiah 14:12

Still, there is no record of when this event took place, but we
do know that Satan was already in the Garden of Eden with Adam
and Eve. A careful study of Scripture points to Lucifer's fall having
occurred sometime after the original creation in Genesis 1:1, and
the condition of the earth as found in Genesis 1:2,

> *"And the earth was formless and void, and darkness was*
> *over the surface of the deep; and the Spirit of God was*
> *moving over the surface of the waters."*

How many years, perhaps millions, took place between these
verses, and what occurred during this time is unknown. In a vision
the prophet Jeremiah saw the earth in such a condition as found in
Genesis 1:2. In the record of that vision are the causes which led
up to a cataclysmic annihilation of life on the entire planet,

> *"I looked on the earth, and, behold, it was formless and*
> *void; and to the heavens, and they had no light. I looked*
> *on the mountains, and, behold, they were quaking, and*
> *all the hills moved to and fro. I looked, and, behold, there*
> *was no man, and all the birds of the heavens had fled.*
> *I looked, and behold, the fruitful land was a wilderness,*
> *and all its cities were pulled down before the Lord, before*
> *His fierce anger. For thus says the Lord, 'The whole*

*land shall be a desolation, yet I will not execute a
complete destruction. For this the earth shall mourn, and
the heavens above be dark, because I have spoken, I have
purposed, and I will not change My mind, nor will I turn
from it.' "*

Jeremiah 4:23-28

This desolation was a direct result of the Lord's fierce anger,
but why was He angry? Sometime during the vast time span between
the original creation and the destruction, Satan, with one third of
all the angels, was cast into the earth. He had so perverted God's
creation that it had to be completely destroyed. Let us consider the
description of the earth as found in Genesis 1:2 and the one described
in this prophetic vision of Jeremiah. They are nearly identical. True
to His Word, God did not make a full end, but began again, as seen
in Genesis 1:3. Science actually supports the details of creation in
the Bible.

There is one final point of interest that should not be ignored.
After God created Adam and Eve He gave them a specific command
to "be fruitful and multiply, and *replenish* the earth..." (Genesis
1:22). How could they replenish the earth unless it had once before
been filled? We need not be deceived by the lies and tricks of the
devil; he will go to any length to cause us to doubt the authenticity
of God's Word, to subvert His authority and ultimately, to destroy
our worship of Him. A. W. Tozer had a straightforward view of
such matters,

> *"Science of course deals with the relation of things and
> their effect upon each other. But the plain people, the
> people who would rather believe than to know, and who
> would rather worship than to discover - they have a
> simpler and more beautiful view of the world."*[47]

Occult

What comes to mind when we think of the occult? Millions of
Americans saw a movie that came out in the early seventies called,
"The Exorcist," which focused on a case of demon possession.

However representative of Satan's work as the movie may be, the devil will usually pose in much more subtle and attractive ways. An article appeared in the June 8, 1987 issue of "Insight: The Washington Times," about modern-day witches that presented just such a disguised view.

In this article, some very disturbing misconceptions were put forth that attempted to separate witchcraft from Satan. The following are some quotes from letters printed in response to the article,

> *"Avoiding the false Hollywood stereotypes and correctly disassociating both witches and their religion from satanism, the article presented a view of their religion that is believable..."*

> *"Witchcraft is flourishing because of its positive benefits to its participants and the entire planet. Most rituals have some focus on healing our ravaged Mother Earth. Women especially are drawn to it because of the emphasis on a female divinity which has been denied us in all Western religions.*
>
> *I find it appalling that satanism is mentioned in the glossary of witchcraft terms. Satan has nothing to do with witchcraft, wicca or paganism. None of these groups even believe in the devil's existence. Most feel that Satan is a figment of the medieval church's collective imagination used to coerce people into becoming tithe-giving churchgoers."*

We should make no mistake about these things. Behind all forms of the occult, whether under the guise of religion or not, lies the devil himself. The Word of God is quite clear as to who we are to worship and equally clear as to what occultish practices we should avoid,

> *"There shall not be found among you anyone who makes his son or his daughter pass through the fire, one who uses divination, one who practices witchcraft, or one who interprets omens, or a sorcerer, or one who casts a spell,*

or a medium or a spiritist, or one who calls up the dead.
For whoever does these things is detestable to the Lord;
and because of these detestable things the Lord your God
will drive them out before you.''

Deuteronomy 18:12-14

This passage covers many such activities that today may go unrecognized and may even be accepted as harmless. Tragically, this is not the case. Even something as seemingly innocent as reading the daily horoscopes is a dangerous practice. In addition to astrology, there are warnings against palm reading, fortune-telling, using ouija boards, going to seances, and attempting to speak to the dead. All of this is forbidden in the Bible, including of course, blatant Satan worship. Sin of this nature was not tolerated because it was a direct affront against the omnipotence of God by the original thief himself, the father of lies. The punishment for these practices was severe,

''He who sacrifices to any god, other than to the Lord
alone, shall be utterly destroyed.''

Exodus 22:20

Although we are no longer under the law, God's principles are still the same; His standards have not been lowered just because we now live under the dispensation of grace. If we are to become true worshippers of the living God, there must be no doors through which Satan may gain an entrance into our lives. An idol does not become an idol overnight; it takes time. What may have at first appeared to be an innocent practice or a fun game may lead to the bondage of idolatry. Let us use wisdom, trust in God and allow the Holy Spirit to steer us clear of every dangerous practice.

''...one of the obvious contrasts between response to the
demonic and response to the Divine is that the demonic
prefers a mindlessness or trance, but God always
demands an active mind and will. Relationship with God
in worship is for the entire person - spirit, soul and body
- and we are invited to be willing and active participants
in that experience.''[48]

Chapter 11

Gratefully We Serve

If we were to make a totally honest appraisal of ourselves, what would our answer be to the following questions? How appreciative are we of God's unspeakable gift? Do we, like Monarch, the grateful dog in the opening story, respond to our Master with exuberant anticipation and a desire to please? Can others see, from looking at our day-to-day lives, that we are motivated by an all-consuming love for God? Are we a light burning in this darkened world?

Worship involves our giving to God. We present to Him a gift in thankfulness for who He is and what He has done,

> *"The Lord has done great things for us; we are glad."*
>
> Psalm 126:3

What can we give to the Lord, that He doesn't already have? He owns the cattle on a thousand hills and the earth itself, in all its fullness. What more is left? The greatest thing we can give to God is what He gave to us - our entire life, placing ourselves in His service. As we saw in the tabernacle, we are to be living sacrifices. Paul wrote in Romans that this sacrifice leads not to death, but to a new life of service,

> *"I urge you therefore, brethren, by the mercies of God to present your bodies a living and holy sacrifice, acceptable to God, which is your **spiritual service of worship**."*
>
> Romans 12:1

What does the God of the whole universe want with our

135

bodies? He wants them to be washed in the blood of the Lamb, filled with His Spirit and consecrated to serve in holiness.

Although He desires for us to soar in the spiritual abandonment of worship, we must still be down to earth (another antinomy). It is important to not become "so heavenly minded that we are of no earthly good." Mountaintops of praise and worship enable us to return to the valleys and *be loving servants*!

Ronald Allen and Gordon Borror aptly noted,

> *"How are we fully to love one another as Christ loved us if we do not practice loving God? How can we possibly love lost mankind except to see them as God sees them? We cannot see from His point of view until we know Him."*[49]

As we submit to the role of ministering to others in love, having developed within us the heart attitudes of a true servant, we become more like Jesus,

> *"...whoever wishes to become great among you shall be your servant; and whoever wishes to be first among you shall be slave of all. For even the Son of Man did not come to be served, but to serve, and to give His life a ransom for many."*
>
> Mark 10:43-45

All of our service must be directed from a heart that acknowledges the glory, majesty and power of One who is the *King*, yet who came to *serve*. Our ministry must not stem from a dead obedience to an Almighty Entity; rather, our spirits should radiate the joy of our salvation in all of our work. True service will enable us to worship in everything we do, which in turn, leads to a greater desire to continue serving. "The joy of the Lord is our strength" (Nehemiah 8:10).

When we come to the point that the joy of the Lord *is* our strength, we will experience a spiritual abandonment that separates us from the anxieties of the world. No longer will fear and frustration keep us bound to false conceptions of worship and distorted views of

Christian service. As we achieve a measure of spiritual maturity, cold, ritualistic religion with its "good deed-doing" will melt under a heart aflame. Fiery worship gives birth to genuine, worshipful service springing forth out of a purified heart.

Herein lies the key to grateful service. It can in no way take the place of worship, rather, results from it. There is a divine order to be observed. We see this association between worship and service in the words of Jesus during His temptation in the wilderness,

> *Begone, Satan! For it is written, 'You shall **worship** the Lord your God, and **serve** Him only.''*
>
> Matthew 4:10

As we have seen, worship is a spontaneous and dynamic expression of heartfelt emotion. It is a response on our part to God's greatness - or as someone once said, "the occupation of the heart, not with its needs or even with its blessings but with God, Himself." Can we proclaim with King David,

> *"And again what more can David say to Thee? For Thou knowest Thy **servant**, O Lord God! For the sake of Thy word, and according to Thine own heart, Thou hast done all this greatness to let Thy servant know. For this reason Thou art great, O Lord God; for there is none like Thee, and there is no God besides Thee, according to all that we have heard with our ears."*
>
> II Samuel 7:20-22

Can we rest in His presence as we allow Him to create in us a pure servant's heart? Any other form of service is but a mere human copy that will fade away. In comparison, "The work done by a worshipper will have eternity in it."[50]

A word of warning in order that we not be deceived: people of the world frequently attempt to duplicate the fruits of the Spirit, using them to further their own ambitions. The genuine fruits - love, joy, peace, long-suffering, gentleness, meekness and temperance are a result of the crucifixion of the flesh with all its affections and lusts.

The world, in its attempt to mimic these fruits, puts forth a facade, sort of a whitewashed fence, for others to see. They place a nice, external covering over their old selves. There is no inner heart change, just a hiding of the imperfections inherent in the old nature. Sincerity is sadly lacking. If we study some background on the word "sincere", it will give us a better understanding of such counterfeits.

Sincerity is related to a phrase "sin cero," meaning "without wax." In ancient times, when a sculpture was completed with no imperfections, there would be no need for wax to give a smooth appearance. If there were cracks or chips, then melted wax was applied to hide the fact that the marble was not "true." Of course, the most expensive sculptures, by reputable craftsmen, were marked "sin cero." We, as Christians, need true sincerity in our walk through worship and communion with the Lord. In His holy presence, the false is exposed to us and sanctified through repentance. Father, keep us from becoming another polished apple with a rotten core!

True ministry, then, is accomplished through the anointing of the Holy Spirit. As our worship experience develops, our capacity for service expands and we become an extension of His love. His gifts are better able to flow through us to the surrounding world, effecting changes in it. "Truly, those who worship most will serve God best, and only the Spirit can supply the power for both."[51]

God the Father, in His ultimate wisdom, has made allowance for our weaknesses. He has given to every believer all he or she will ever need to serve Him. When we come to God it is in our weakness, which is exactly as He wants it to be. We are not to labor in our own strength or to depend solely upon innate abilities. How, then, are we to accomplish the work given to us? In the book of Zechariah we find God's answer, which is equally as true for us today,

> "...This is the word of the Lord to Zerubbabel saying, 'Not by might nor by power, but **by My Spirit**,' says the Lord of hosts."
>
> Zechariah 4:6

We have already seen that God the Father desires His children to continue the work of building the Church through the anointing and gifts of the Holy Spirit. In the Church, Christ's spiritual body, just as with the physical body, there is one head - Jesus,

> *"He also is head of the body, the church, and He is the beginning, the first-born from the dead; so that He Himself might come to have first place in everything."*
> Colossians 1:18

For the shepherding and perfecting of His body, Jesus established certain governmental offices, commonly referred to as the "fivefold ministry." These are, as Paul enumerated in his letter to the Ephesian church, the apostle, prophet, evangelist, pastor and teacher. As we know, not everyone is called to be the pastor of a church, or a great evangelist like Billy Graham, yet we are all called to serve and given at least one supernatural gift to compensate for our weakness,

> *"Now there are varieties of gifts, but the **same Spirit**. And there are varieties of ministries, and the **same Lord**. And there are varieties of effects, but the **same God** who works all things in all persons. But to each one is given the manifestation of the Spirit for the common good. For to one is given the word of wisdom through the Spirit, and to another the word of knowledge according to the same Spirit; to another faith by the same Spirit, and to another gifts of healing by the one Spirit. And to another the effecting of miracles, and to another prophecy, and to another the distinguishing of spirits, to another various kinds of tongues, and to another the interpretation of tongues. But one and the same Spirit works all these things, distributing to each one individually just as He wills."*
> I Corinthians 12:4-11

> *"For just as we have many members in one body and all the members do not have the same function, so we, who are many, are one body in Christ, and individually members one of another. And since we have gifts that*

differ according to the grace given to us, let each exercise them accordingly...''

Romans 12:4-6

As Christians, there is a certain unity that exists among us, but yet, we do not become carbon copies of one another. The Spirit enhances, but never dominates our individual role. He helps all to become productive members of a healthy spiritual body which performs the work of Christ in the world.

When others view the living, vibrant Church the power of Jesus should be evident for all to see. It is not something for which we can claim any credit. Instead, as we yield to the Lordship of Jesus Christ, His Spirit will work through us. Thus, Christian service of this sort is a result of our partnership with God, of our union with His Spirit and not of human strength,

*"For we are the true circumcision, who worship in the Spirit of God and glory in Christ Jesus and **put no confidence in the flesh**.''*

Philippians 3:3

Remembering the verse, ''...by My Spirit, says the Lord of Hosts,'' it cannot be over-emphasized that *a lifestyle of worship is the well-spring from which loving, dynamic Christian service flows*. No longer is there a drudgery of obligation to which we feel driven in order to have a clear conscience. Rather, it bubbles out of our innermost being in gratitude to our precious Lord. Let us rejoice in our union with the Lord Jesus. He is the Fountainhead of this mighty roaring river of life. We can be confident in *His* ability to fulfill all that He has promised!

Chapter 12

Truly Transformed

Christian worship is the most momentous, the most urgent, the most glorious action that can take place in human life.''

Karl Barth

This is the heart attitude of every person who is a true worshipper of God. No longer is our worship controlled by the routine of living, taking place only in the first few moments of each church service, but it is the hub around which our life revolves. Neither is it merely, as Bob Mumford stated, ''outward spiritual calisthenics without inwardly worshipping at all.'' As we well know, this transformation does not take place quickly or easily, but no one who has come into the presence of Almighty God has ever left untouched by His hand.

> *"In holy intimacy, the true worshipper comes face to face with God and he is transformed by the glory. If the corporate worship in the church leaves people unchanged, the church is not really worshipping. If what goes on in a church service does not spur the saints to greater obedience, call it what you will, it isn't worship. Worship always results in a transformation and the church is edified by it.''*[52]

When Moses approached the burning bush in answer to the call of God, He was forever changed and given a great purpose in life. The prophet Isaiah was another who looked up to see the glory of God and was changed. He became the most well-known Old Testament prophet because of the revelation given him of the coming of the Messiah. Ezekiel saw God's glory and became the prophet and watchman of Israel. Each change came after they had seen the glory of the Lord. The same is true for us today.

Once we have set our heart to become a worshipper, the process of transformation begins. This is the time during which we come to acknowledge that the hunger within can only be filled by God and some of the rough exterior is smoothed out. Then one day, while looking up, we too, are given a glimpse of the glory of the Lord. Seeing the "utter and awesome holiness of God," and "ourselves against the backdrop of that holiness," our lives cannot help but be forever changed.[53]

The apostle Paul is a prime example of this metamorphosis. With misguided zeal, he persecuted the early believers and even had authorization from the highest Jewish officials for the task. One day, Saul, as he was then called, had an experience on the road to Damascus that changed him completely. He met Jesus (Acts 9:3-6). This was the beginning of a life of true worship for the man who would come to write the greater portion of the New Testament.

In review, worship is the motivational aspect of our relationship with God that keeps the fires of our heart burning brightly, regardless of the circumstances in which we may find ourselves. In worship, the spirit soars heavenward and, though our lives may be filled with physical suffering, we are able to rejoice in all things. Passionate, fiery *worship,* when balanced with a well-founded *knowledge* and steadfast *covenant* with God, makes the following promise a reality,

> *"But in all these things we overwhelmingly conquer through Him who loved us."*
>
> Romans 8:37

Paul could say this with such confidence because he had learned this truth from experience,

> *"...in far more labors, in far more imprisonments, beaten times without number, often in danger of death. Five times I received from the Jews thirty-nine lashes, three times I was beaten with rods, once I was stoned, three*

*times I was shipwrecked, a night and a day I have spent
in the deep. I have been on frequent journeys, in dangers
from rivers, dangers from robbers, dangers from my
countrymen, dangers from the Gentiles, dangers in the
city, dangers in the wilderness, dangers on the sea,
dangers among false brethren; I have been in labor and
hardship, through many sleepless nights, in hunger and
thirst, often without food, in cold and exposure...''*

II Corinthians 11:23-27

Throughout all these tribulations Paul was able to declare,
''Rejoice evermore'' (I Thessalonians 5:16). His worship remained
steadfast in each of the various mountains and valleys through which
his walk with the Lord carried him.

As our life of worship progresses from glory to glory and we
discover what it means to abide in God's presence, the Holy Spirit
will bring forth fruit. These spiritual fruits are listed in Paul's writings
we mentioned earlier, ''love, joy, peace, long-suffering, gentleness,
goodness, faith, meekness, temperance...'' (Galatians 5:22,23)

In the words of Jesus,

*I am the vine, you are the branches; he who abides in
Me, and I in him, he bears much fruit; for apart from
Me you can do nothing...If you abide in Me, and My
words abide in you, ask whatever you wish, and it shall
be done for you. By this is My Father glorified, that you
bear much fruit, and prove to be My disciples.''*

John 15:5,7,8

In many ways, the transformation that occurs in us is similar
to the process in which a stone, in the hands of a master sculptor,
becomes a work of art. Michelangelo, perhaps the greatest sculptor
of all time, once described his talents as an ability to see the
masterpiece hidden within the block of marble, and then to release
it. God the Father sees that perfect worshipping servant contained
within our rough exteriors. As we, through our worship, abide in
Jesus the Holy Spirit brings forth another masterpiece.

Coupled with this freedom to worship comes a greater

responsibility and renewed call to holiness. It was *only after* God commanded Moses to build a tabernacle, the pattern for all true worship, that He said, "You shall be holy, for I the Lord your God am holy" (Leviticus 19:2). This call to holiness cannot be fulfilled until we learn to worship.

Erwin Lutzer, author of *Failure - The Back Door to Success*, discussed the advantages of occasional setbacks. As God leads us toward holiness we will fail, but such times of reversal can be used to develop character if viewed from the proper perspective. Quietly and patiently enduring, continuing to rise and rejoicing evermore in our total dependency upon God causes our lives to become a pleasing fragrance to Him. We need not become frustrated or discouraged because of newly-discovered shortcomings. Rather, we can take heart in God's faithfulness and draw near to Him. In His presence is fullness of joy and at His right hand are pleasures forevermore (Psalm 16:11).

Yes, worship accomplishes great things for God, both in and through the believer. Before Lucifer (the light-bearer fell from heaven, one of his duties as the anointed cherub was to lead the hosts of heaven in their worship of the Father. Why has he now, as Satan, gone to such great lengths to distort the truth of this glorious encounter? Why has it been his desire to make believers apprehensive about coming into the presence of Almighty God? The answer is very simple. Satan knows the power of worship.

> *"The fuel of worship is a true vision of the greatness of God; the fire that makes the fuel burn white-hot is the quickening of the Holy Spirit; the furnace made alive and warm by the flame of truth is our renewed spirit; the resulting heat of our affections is powerful worship, pushing its way out in confessions, longings, acclamations, tears, songs, shouts, bowed heads, lifted hands and obedient lives.*"[54]

On the day that the body of Christ begins to worship God as He desires, we will experience the greatest move of the Holy Spirit this world has ever imagined. Satan will do everything he can to prevent this from happening, but he is doomed to failure. It is promised that when the Bridegroom returns to receive His Bride *she will be spotless*! Through *perfected love - worship*, based on *knowledge*, leading to *covenant* with God - this will be accomplished.

Shall we take one last look into the heavenlies, that the fire blazing in our heart may intensify?

Chapter 13

When Time Draws to a Close

In "Visions of Glory" God the Father was seated on the heavenly throne. Jesus was revealed both as the Lamb and the soon-coming King. We witnessed, with John, the countless thousands worshipping in the most magnificent service ever assembled. There is yet one scene to be unveiled in our heavenward gaze - the spectacle that will take place at the beginning of God's judgment,

> *"And when He broke the seventh seal, there was* ***silence*** *in heaven for about half an hour."*
>
> Revelation 8:1

Perhaps some of us have wondered what significance this holds in God's plan. God has commanded that we "be still and know that He is God." At the beginning of judgment is the absolute and utter fulfillment of this Scripture. Every being in heaven, in earth and under the earth - even Satan - will be silent when God the Father rises from His throne to pronounce judgment. For one half hour every eye will be riveted on the Father as He stands in all of His unimaginable glory.

In the book of Psalms is the first clue to this ultimate revelation,

> *"Thou didst cause judgment to be heard from heaven; the earth feared, and was still, when God arose to judgment, to save all the humble of the earth."*
>
> Psalms 76:8,9

147

The Lord revealed to the prophet Daniel the wonders that will follow,

> *"I kept looking, and that horn was waging war with the saints and overpowering them **until** the Ancient of Days came, and judgment was passed in favor of the saints of the Highest One, and the time arrived when the saints took possession of the kingdom."*
>
> Daniel 7:21,22

After God the Father stands, He will come to the throne of judgment to assume His rightful place,

> *"I kept looking until thrones were set up, and the Ancient of Days took His seat; His vesture was like white snow, and the hair of His head like pure wool, His throne was ablaze with flames, its wheels were a burning fire. A river of fire was flowing and coming out from before Him; thousands upon thousands were attending Him, and myriads upon myriads were standing before Him. The court sat, and the books were opened."*
>
> Daniel 7:9,10

Silence.   *Awesome, deafening quiet.*

So great is our glorious God, that countless numbers will be speechless before Him in heaven. The Father is preparing us for that last day. He is teaching us to worship Him in reverential wonder, and yet, in intimate gratitude - like the spontaneous joy of Monarch in our opening story. There is only one question. *Will we respond*?

APPENDIX I
Bibliography

Holy Bible, New American Standard Version: The Lockman Foundation and Thomas Nelson Publishers, 1977.

Allen, Ronald & Borror, Gordon. *Worship - Rediscovering the Missing Jewel*: Multnomah Press, 1982.

Cornwall, Judson. *Elements of Worship*: Bridge Publishing, Inc., 1985.

Cornwall, Judson. *Let Us Worship*: Bridge Publishing, Inc., 1983.

Gibbs, Alfred P. *Worship, The Christian's Highest Occupation:* Walterick Publications, n.d.

Jennings, Theodore W. *Life as Worship*: Wm. B. Eerdmans Publishing Co., 1982.

MacArthur, John F. *The Ultimate Priority*: Moody Press, 1983.

Mears, Henrietta C. *What the Bible is All About:* Regal, 1983.

Mumford, Bob. *Entering and Enjoying Worship*: Manna Christian Outreach, 1975.

Nee, Watchman. *The Spiritual Man*: Christian Fellowship Publishers, Inc., 1968.

Pink, Arthur W. *Profiting from the Word*: The Banner of Truth Trust, 1985.

Piper, John. *Desiring God*: Multnomah Press, 1986.

Ravenhill, Leonard. *Revival Praying*: Bethany House, 1962.

Taylor, Jack R. *The Hallelujah Factor*: Broadman Press, 1983.

Tozer, A.W. *Worship: The Missing Jewel of the Evangelical Church*: Christian Publications.

Wiersbe, Warren W. *Real Worship*: Oliver Nelson, 1986.

APPENDIX II
Notes

Part I

1. A.P. Gibbs, *Worship, The Christian's Highest Occupation* (Walterick Publications, n.d.), pp. 63-64.
2. A.W. Tozer, *Worship, The Missing Jewel of the Evangelical Church* (Christian Publications, n.d.), p. 11.
3. Blaise Pascal, *Pascal's Pensees,* trans. by W.F. Trotter (E.P. Dutton, 1958), p. 113.
4. Judson Cornwall, *Let Us Worship* (Bridge Publishing, Inc., 1985), p. 11.
5. Judson Cornwall, *The Elements of Worship* (Bridge Publishing, Inc., 1983), pp. 11-12.
6. Tozer, *Worship, The Missing Jewel of the Evangelical Church,* title.
7. Cornwall, *Let Us Worship,* p. 51.
8. Tozer, *Worship, The Missing Jewel of the Evangelical Church,* pp.7-9.
9. William Temple, *The Hope of a New World,* p. 30, cited by Allen & Borror, *Worship, Rediscovering the Missing Jewel,* (Multnomah Press, 1982), p. 39.
10. John F. MacArthur, *The Ultimate Priority* (Moody Press, 1983), p. 87.
11. Tozer, *Worship, The Missing Jewel of the Evangelical Church,* p. 9.
12. Cornwall, *Let Us Worship,* p. 45.
13. John Piper, *Desiring God* (Multnomah Press, 1986), p. 65.
14. Chuck Swindoll, Message Series, ''Growing Deep in the Christian Life'' (Insight for Living, Fullerton, California, 1987).
15. Gibbs, *Worship, The Christian's Highest Occupation,* p. 51.

Part II

16. Cornwall, *Elements of Worship,* p. 199.
17. Bob Mumford, *Entering and Enjoying Worship* (Manna Christian Outreach, 1975), preface.
18. Piper, *Desiring God,* p. 67.
19. Gibbs, *Worship, The Christian's Highest Occupation,* pp. 157-176, 189-199.
20. MacArthur, *The Ultimate Priority,* p. 79.
21. Cornwall, *Let Us Worship,* p. 172.
22. Henrietta C. Mears, *What the Bible is All About* (Regal, 1983).
23. Cornwall, *Elements of Worship,* p. 99.
24. Theodore W. Jennings, *Life As Worship* Wm. B. Eerdmans Publishing Co., 1982), p. 65.
25. Cornwall, *Elements of Worship,* p. 82.
26. Leonard Ravenhill, *Revival Praying* (Bethany House Publishers, 1962). in "Last Days Magazine" (Last Days Ministries, Fall 1987), p. 26.
27. Arthur W. Pink, *Profiting from the Word* (The Banner of Truth Trust, 1985), p. 51.
28. Ibid, p. 52.
29. Ibid, p. 49.
30. Jennings, *Life As Worship,* p. 67.

Part III

31. Allen & Borror, *Worship, Rediscovering the Missing Jewel,* p. 132.
32. Cornwall, *Elements of Worship,* p. 113.
33. Cornwall, *Let Us Worship,* p. 33.
34. Allen & Borror, *Worship, Rediscovering the Missing Jewel,* pp. 23-24.
35. Ibid, p. 19.
36. Ibid, p. 189.
37. Jennings, *Life As Worship,* preface.
38. Cornwall, *Elements of Worship,* p. 108.
39. MacArthur, *The Ultimate Priority,* pp. 121-122.
40. Warren Wiersbe, *Real Worship* (Oliver Nelson, 1986), p. 180.
41. Gibbs, *Worship, The Christian's Highest Occupation,* p. 17.
42. Mumford, *Entering and Enjoying Worship,* p. 25.
43. Gibbs, *Worship, The Christian's Highest Occupation,* p. 216.
44. Ibid, p. 233.
45. Cornwall, *Elements of Worship,* p. 116.
46. Gibbs, *Worship, The Christian's Highest Occupation,* p. 145.
47. Tozer, *Worship, The Missing Jewel of the Evangelical Church,* pp. 5-6
48. Cornwall, *Elements of Worship,* p. 117.
49. Allen & Borror, *Worship, Rediscovering the Missing Jewel,* p. 38.
50. Tozer, *Worship, The Missing Jewel of the Evangelical Church,* p. 14.
51. Gibbs, *Worship, The Christian's Highest Occupation,* p. 199.
52. MacArthur, *The Ultimate Priority,* p. 155.
53. Ibid, p. 86.
54. Piper, *Desiring God,* p. 66.

Dr. Gills has provided this book at no charge, but you are encouraged to make a tax-deductible contribution of any amount to either the **CATARACT TEACHING FOUNDATION** or one of his preferred charities, **TRINITY COLLEGE.**

About The CATARACT TEACHING FOUNDATION

Dr. Gills founded this non-profit organization to assist and train ophthalmologists in developing nations. Contributions help to expand the foundation's program which provides teaching instruction, low cost equipment and surgery to the people of nations less blessed than ours. Through a combined effort with the Christian Medical Society, they completed and equipped the first teaching facility in the Dominican Republic. Other developing nations view this facility as the "model" to follow.

Each one of your dollars will effect $10.00 worth of benefits in these nations. Contributions are tax deductible under IRS Code 509 (A)(1). The Federal Tax Exempt Number is 59-2335816. Please make your checks payable to:

THE CATARACT TEACHING FOUNDATION
1570 U.S. 19 N; P.O. Box 5000
Tarpon Springs, FL 34688-5000

About TRINITY COLLEGE

Dr. William T. Watson founded Trinity College in 1932. To date, the most widely known graduate of Trinity is Dr. Billy Graham, who has attained world reknown through his anointed evangelical ministry.

Trinity College is a school that emphasizes the preparation of young people for effective Christian ministry. "The educational philosophy of Trinity College is Biblical, evangelical, growth-oriented and service oriented," and views the practical application of God's truth as its goal.

Trinity College is licensed by the State Board of Independent Colleges and Universities of the State of Florida, and is chartered under Florida law. Also, Trinity is a member of The Evangelical Teacher Training Association and is now in applicant status with the American Association of Bible Colleges.

Please make tax deductible financial gifts to this charity payable to Trinity College Scholarship Fund, addressed as follows:

TRINITY COLLEGE SCHOLARSHIP FUND
c/o Barry L. Banther, President
Box 877
Dunedin, Florida 34296